INSIGHT COMPACT GUIDE

Copenhagen

GREAT LITTLE GUIDES

Compact Guide: Copenhagen is the ideal quick-reference guide to Denmark's lively capital. From the buzz of the city's jazz clubs to the fun of Tivoli Gardens, from the legacy of Hans Christian Andersen to the radical lifestyle of Christiania, it's all here.

This is one of almost 100 titles in *Apa Publications'* innovative series of pocket-sized, easy-to-use guide-books intended for the independent-minded traveller. *Compact Guides* are in essence travel encyclopedias in miniature, designed to be comprehensive yet portable, as well as up-to-date and authoritative.

Star Attractions

An instant reference to some of Copenhagen's top attractions to help you set your priorities.

Rådhuspladsen p14

Tivoli Gardens p16

Carlsberg Brewery p23

National Museum p26

State Art Museum p39

Rosenberg Slot p40

Royal Life Guard p44

Nyhavn p47

Bakken fun park p65

Louisiana Museum of Modern Art p68

Roskilde Cathedral p70

COPENHAGEN

Introduction

Places

Culture

Leisure

Practical Information

Copenhagen: Scandinavia's Liveliest Capital

When Denmark briefly ruled all of Scandinavia, Copenhagen was the capital of Norway and Sweden as well. The Danes still like to regard the city as the region's most important and cosmopolitan city.

Copenhagen occupies a delightful spot by the Øresund; the waters of this narrow link between the Baltic and the Kattegat flow right past the heart of the city via a series of man-made canals and natural channels. Although most of the docks and quayside installations have gone for good, the maritime atmosphere is ever-present, and indeed the best way to get a first feel of the city is from the water. But Copenhagen is also very much a walking city, the first European capital to be developed with an understanding of the pleasure of strolling through streets free of motor cars and exhaust fumes. The casual pace of the crowds extends to the city's delightful parks and open spaces – favoured venues for picnics and recreation. Children and young people are not restricted by signs and by-laws and adults appreciate the informality that is so much a part of the Danish character. In fact, it is the friendliness and openness of the Copenhageners that has helped to make the city so popular as a holiday destination.

Nyhavn waterfront

Copenhagen's varied cultural calendar has something for everyone: paintings and sculptures for the art enthusiast, avant-garde and alternative lifestyles for the younger generation and the fairy tales of Hans Christian Andersen for children. Whether it is classical music or rock music, art or literature, museums or open-air sculpture that draws you to Copenhagen, the choice is broad for deciding how to spend your time.

Few would dispute that Copenhagen is the liveliest of the Scandinavian capitals, with something going on every day and night. It would be a shame to try to cram everything that this wonderful city has to offer into a weekend. If possible, try to allow a few more days to savour its intriguing mixture of big-city jungle and quiet backwaters.

5

Rådhusplasden

Location and size

The Danish capital is located on the 55th parallel at about the same distance from the equator as Glasgow and Moscow. Copenhagen lies on the eastern side of the Baltic Sealand island and opposite the northern end of the island of Amager. The Øresund, here about 16km (10 miles) wide, separates Sealand and Amager in the west from the Swedish mainland in the east. From earliest times, the Sund has been the main waterway between the Baltic and the Kattegat. The population of

Copenhagen itself is about 465,000, the separate entity of Frederiksberg 85,000. Add in the outlying suburbs and greater Copenhagen's numbers rise to about 1.7 million.

Climate and when to go

A maritime position in a temperate climate zone generally means stable temperatures but changing weather patterns. A week of unbroken sunshine is rare, but that is actually more likely than seven days of persistent rain. Light rainwear is always advisable, with umbrellas often unsuitable in the strong winds.

If you want to explore Copenhagen's open spaces and take lots of walks around the city, then you can rely on warm or at least adequate temperatures from May through to September.

Museums and indoor entertainment in the Danish capital can be enjoyed at any time of the year. But outdoor types need not necessarily shun the wet and windy months from November onwards. Tourists are few and far between during the winter and accommodation is much, much cheaper.

The language

Foreigners who make an attempt to speak the language of their hosts are always well received. However, the Danes speak very quickly and often drop not only letters but also syllables, so well-meaning but inexperienced tourists, after having been asked a simple question in a café three times, may well abandon their attempts to emulate the natives. Most Danes can, after all, make themselves understood perfectly well in English. Despite these pronunciation difficulties, saying the little word *tak* ('thank you') is always appreciated.

The Danish language has some letters of its own: Æ and æ correspond roughly with 'e' as in 'end', Ø and ø with 'er' in 'fern', while Å and å (sometimes written as 'Aa or 'aa') is a long, open sound.

The city's development and layout

Copenhagen's historic centre lies close to the Sund between Sealand and North Amager. The present straight shorelines on both sides of the islands are of artificial origin. Over the past 700 years, millions of tree-trunks have been driven into the mud, so that castles and palaces, homes and factories could be built.

The first castle was built by Bishop Absalon of Roskilde in 1167, on the small island of Holmen just off the west bank of the Sund. Around it the settlement of Købmandshavn grew up. The Holmen power base later became Slotsholmen and, on the site of the present Old Town, Købmandshavn grew into København.

Until 1856, ramparts, now Vester Voldgade, Nørre Voldgade and Østre Voldgade, surrounded the Old Town. To call the area within the old ramparts the Old Town is only partially true, as several large fires destroyed many original buildings and, during the 1960s and '70s, there were some thoughtless *ad hoc* developments. Nevertheless, most museums, palaces, hotels, bars, restaurants and shopping streets are concentrated in this area. From 1968 onwards, much of the central area was converted into a traffic-free zone and so very little of this quarter can now be described as residential.

Canoeing at Slotsholmen

When, in the middle of the 19th century, impoverished workers poured into the already overcrowded town, it was decided to clear away the ramparts. On the other side of the old fortifications, speculators began to build mainly multi-storey tenements containing small, cramped flats with rear courtyards, but these quickly became slums. In accordance with their position beside the course of the old ramparts, the districts in this new quarter bear the names Nørrebro, Vesterbro and Østerbro.

A more relaxing pursuit

7

As industry declined after World War II, these typically working-class quarters gradually became the catchment area for those people who couldn't afford anything better. But, given the poor state of the dwellings, they cried out for redevelopment. Nørrebro, the oldest quarter, was the first part of the city to come under the scrutiny of the town planners, but unfortunately no grand plan was devised. So the inhabitants of Nørrebro defended themselves stoutly and, during the 1960s and '70s, the otherwise peace-loving city of Copenhagen became the scene of determined house occupations and fierce street battles.

In the end, the sceptics saw their worst fears confirmed. Initially, the newly-designed blocks looked good, but newcomers arrived and the original inhabitants were forced to move out. When redevelopment work started in Vesterbro *(see pages 21–24)*, care was taken to avoid the same mistakes. The situation was rather different in Østerbro as this district wasn't as old as the other two. As well as the old working-class settlements, there are also streets with spacious houses and the residents represent a significantly wider class spectrum.

A spruced-up Vesterbro

Frederiksberg has not faced this sort of problem. Although this area adjoins Vesterbro and Nørrebro, it forms a town within a town. It has its own district council and its own town hall. Like many other buildings in Frederiksberg, the town hall is rather grand, although the population represents a fair cross-section of the community.

The more affluent residential areas begin north of Østerbro. Hellerup, Charlottenlund and Klampenborg are newer, compact settlements, where grand villas lie hidden behind tall hedges and gates. These quarters are part of the

Christiana Free State graffiti

View from the Vor Frelsers Kirke

Gentofte and Lyngby districts, both renowned as areas for very wealthy Copenhageners. Further north lie extensive open spaces, lakes and streams.

For the inhabitants of the satellite towns to the south of the city, such leafy luxury can only be a dream. The long, coastal strip between Brøndby Strand and Køge is dominated by large residential blocks and oil tanks. Attempts are underway to make this part of greater Copenhagen more attractive.

There is no need for any facelifts in Christianshavn. Here, on the northern tip of Amager, the clock seems to tick more slowly – a fact that is much appreciated by those who enjoy an alternative lifestyle in the Free State of Christiania *(see pages 55–6)*. While work progresses on the building projects associated with the new Øresund crossing to Sweden, hardly any trace of big-city bustle remains in Christianshavn, as the port has been moved out of the city centre to the northern and southern outskirts, and the docks have been sealed off.

The Queen of Denmark

King Frederik IX only had daughters, so when he died in 1972, one of his brothers would have succeeded to the throne had not the constitution been changed in 1953 to enable Margarethe, the eldest daughter, to succeed in the absence of male heirs.

Royal photo call

Born on 16 April 1940, immediately after the German occupation of Denmark, Margarethe benefited from the popularity of her grandfather, Christian IX, who stayed in the country and was often seen out and about on the streets of Copenhagen. Margarethe II, the intelligent and well-educated queen of a constitutional monarchy, has retained her popularity, even though she has no real power. She has generally refrained from commenting on matters of political sensitivity, but during the mid-1980s she could not ignore the racist attacks and the agitation against asylum seekers, which upset the tolerant Danes. Her statements on human rights started a nationwide debate and she was praised for her intervention, although she did receive abuse from right-wingers.

Her artistic achievements are well documented: she has designed vestments for the church in her summer residence, illustrated books, including J.R.R. Tolkien's *Lord of the Rings*, drawn stamps and, together with her husband, translated Simone de Beauvoir's *Tous les hommes sont mortels* into Danish.

In 1967 she married the French diplomat Henri de Laborde de Monpezat, now Prince Henrik of Denmark. *On guard at Amalienborg* He immediately won the hearts of the people when he made a speech in perfect Danish. Margarethe II and Henrik have two sons: Crown Prince Frederik (born 1968), who works assiduously at his role as heir to the throne, and Prince Joachim (born 1969).

The economy

Services and administration, transport and commerce are the main sources of employment in Copenhagen. The transition from an industrialised economy to a service economy started a long time ago and the gradual demise of the old-style B & W dockyard has only served to underline the huge structural changes that have taken place in the city. In 1996, the last 1,200 dockworkers lost their jobs in a company that was once the biggest private employer in the city. In the same year, the Tuborg brewery in Hellerup relocated its production facilities. To the south of Hellerup lies the modern freight and container port. Now only ferries moor in the city centre harbour. Tourism attracts about 1.8 million visitors every year.

The brewing behemoth

Where to find the city's greats

Although it lies off the beaten track in the Nørrebro district, the Assistens Kirkegård, which is both a cemetery and a park, is included in many organised tours. Because space was at a premium in the overcrowded city during the 18th century, the cemetery (1760) was laid out beyond the ramparts. Many of Copenhagen's celebrities, including Søren Kierkegaard, Christen Købke, Hans Christian Andersen and other famous actors, composers, writers, architects and scientists, are buried here – and this is, of course, what draws the tourists.

During the summer, the cemetery becomes a park and is popular with picnickers. The main entrance is from Kapelvej. Bus no. 5 or 16. Open from May to September, 8am–8pm; November to March, 8am–4pm; otherwise 8am–6pm. Ask for a map in the Tourist Office.

Historical Highlights

1167 King Valdemar the Great gives Bishop Absalon of Roskilde land by the Øresund, which includes the fishing and trading settlement of Havn. Absalon builds a castle on the island of Holmen.

1254 The village of Købmandshavn or 'Merchants' Port' receives a municipal charter. The Hanseatic League, which has risen to power in the Baltic, recognises the expanding port as an important staging post for Baltic trade, but suppresses every attempt to achieve independence, on three occasions resorting to force.

1332–40 Denmark is ruled by the counts of Holstein.

1354 Valdemar IV Atterdag unites the country and restores the throne.

1369 The castle is demolished. It is replaced in 1376 by Copenhagen Castle.

1397 Queen Margrete I of Denmark forges the Kalmar Union, a federation of the Nordic kingdoms of Denmark, Norway and Sweden under Danish leadership.

1417 Erik VII makes Copenhagen his capital and has a palace built in Helsingør.

1425 onwards All ships using the Sound have to pay a toll; though profitable, this results in centuries-long arguments with other powers. Trade flourishes and the population rises from 3,000 to 10,000.

1523–34 Gustav Vasa's coronation as King of Sweden spells the end of the Kalmar Union, though Norway remains part of Denmark.

1536 Christian III declares Protestantism to be the state religion. Royalty and the nobility are the beneficiaries of secularisation. The ordinary people have to cope with poverty and disease.

1546–83 After six epidemics, sanitary conditions in the city are improved.

1588–1648 Christian IV enlarges the town and harbour and commissions the construction of many grand Renaissance-style buildings, including Rosenborg Castle and the old Stock Exchange. Copenhagen flourishes culturally and economically. However, attempts to make Denmark into a great power end in disaster: during the Thirty Years War, Sweden gains much Danish land and by the time of Christian IV's death in 1648, Denmark is ruined.

1648–70 Reign of Frederik III, who plunges the country into war with Sweden again, during which Denmark loses a third of its territory.

1660 Denmark loses its last southern Swedish province to its neighbours across the Øresund. The gates of Copenhagen and the Øresund become the border between the two countries. As a result, fortifications are strengthened.

1665 Frederik III deprives the nobility of power and establishes an hereditary absolute monarchy.

1711 The plague claims 20,000 lives out of a Copenhagen population of 65,000.

1728 A fire destroys half of Copenhagen's housing stock and renders thousands homeless.

1732 Christian VI demolishes Copenhagen Castle as it does not meet his requirements. It is replaced by Christiansborg Palace.

1784 Following far-reaching land reforms introduced during the regency of Crown Prince Frederik, some 60 percent of Danish peasants become landowners.

by 1800 Overseas trade brings prosperity to the merchants, shipping companies and guilds. At the same time, the concept of the Fatherland emerges as the driving force for the 'Golden Age'. From 1815, many important personalities give a boost to the arts and science (*see Culture, pages 73–7*).

1801 During the Napoleonic Wars, an English fleet under the command of Admiral Nelson destroys much of the Danish fleet in Copenhagen harbour. This forces Denmark to renounce the armed neutrality treaty of 1794, which it had entered into with Sweden, Russia and Prussia.

1807 English ships appear off Copenhagen again and demand the surrender of the Danish fleet. This happens after much of Copenhagen has been destroyed in a bombardment. After this the Danes join the continental alliance against England, and suffer further defeats. By 1813 the country is bankrupt.

1814 The victorious powers dissolve the Denmark–Norway double monarchy at the Treaty of Kiel. Norway is ceded to Sweden and Denmark is allowed to keep Iceland, the Faeroe Islands and Greenland.

1814 onwards The impoverished country embarks on a cultural golden age.

1843 The Tivoli Gardens are opened.

1847 The first railway line links Copenhagen with Roskilde.

1848–9 Absolutism ends without a shot being fired. On 4 June 1849, Frederik VII signs a new constitution. Denmark becomes a constitutional monarchy.

1857 The toll for using the Sound is abolished.

1857 onwards The old ramparts are demolished to create space for dwellings. Industrialisation draws in the poor rural population, but many can't find work. By 1900, the population of Copenhagen approaches 400,000.

1864 After the war with Prussia and Austria, Denmark cedes Schleswig, Holstein and Lauenburg to Germany.

1906 Ole Olsen founds the 'Nordisk Films Kompagni', which is still in existence today and said to be the oldest film company in the world.

1907 onwards With two castles destroyed by fire (1795 and 1884), work on the third Christiansborg Palace starts. In 1918, it becomes the seat of the Folketing, the Danish parliament.

1914–18 Denmark remains neutral during World War I.

1915 Far-reaching constitutional reform. Women given the right to vote.

1924 onwards Social Democrats win power. Despite the devastating economic crisis of the 1930s, the framework for new social legislation is put in place.

1940–5 Though wishing to remain neutral during World War II, as it had in 1914–18, Denmark is invaded by the German army on 9 April 1940 and used as a springboard for the subsequent invasion of Norway. Until 1943 the Germans keep their promise not to interfere in Danish internal affairs, and the country is even allowed to retain its own army. This period of cooperation comes to an end in 1943 when the government resigns. Denmark is recognised as one of the Allies. In October 1943 almost the whole of Denmark's Jewish population manages to escape across the Sound to Sweden, narrowly avoiding deportation to the Nazi death camps. An underground war develops between the Danish resistance on the one hand and the Germans and their collaborators on the other, and results in many executions and acts of sabotage.

1945 All of Denmark, apart from Bornholm, is liberated by the British on 5 May.

1950–70 Modern satellite towns spring up around Copenhagen. Today roughly a quarter of Denmark's entire population lives in or near the capital.

1968 onwards Unplanned redevelopment of several older districts leads to house occupations and protests by residents.

1971 Young people occupy abandoned barracks and found Free State of Christiania (*pages 55–6*).

1972 Margrethe II succeeds Frederik IX as Danish monarch.

1978 Denmark becomes a full member of the European Community.

1993 After Denmark votes against the Maastricht Treaty in the 1992 referendum, the Danes accept a revised treaty.

1996 Copenhagen is Cultural Capital of Europe.

1997 The country remains sceptical about European integration and monetary union.

Rådhusplasden

Route 1

Preceding pages: the City of Green Spires

Around the Tivoli

City Hall Square – Louis Tussaud's Wax Museum – Tivolimuseet – Tivoli – Axeltorv – Tycho Brahe Planetarium *See map on pages 16–17*

Tivoli Gardens are a symbol of typical Danish informality. Many Copenhageners have season tickets, as this pleasure park not only bustles with activity during the summer, but also serves as a meeting-place throughout the rest of the year. It has a stage for a symphony orchestra, live performances of jazz, folk and pop music take place in the pubs and cafés, and visitors will have no difficulty finding somewhere to satisfy their hunger. Twice a week from May to September, a magnificent firework display illuminates the night sky. If the Tivoli is not enough for a day out, then there are plenty of other attractions in the area, many of them within a short walk of the gardens. Start out from City Hall Square, an important Copenhagen landmark that is on nearly all the bus routes.

Rådhuspladsen (City Hall Square) is both an institution and a source of controversy. Gatherings and demonstrations, which have moved (or are moving or are supposed to move) the nation, take place here. Colourful neon signs and the digital news read-out provided by *Politiken*, the respected liberal newspaper, emphasise its importance as a focal point. What causes the controversy is not its place at the heart of the nation, but the way the square has been developed. Traffic has been diverted away from the middle of the square and bus stops removed to the sides. New seating and a café lend a calmer feel to the oth-

'Lur Players' near the City Hall

erwise hectic bustle. But what on earth are those tall, dark, elongated constructions, which cover the two travel and admission ticket sales points? The newspapers are full of complaints and explanations. The politicians who were responsible for them suddenly claim they were poorly advised, while the architects think everyone has misunderstood them. In the meantime, the people wait impatiently for the city fathers to resolve the problem.

The huge **City Hall** ❶, which dominates the southeast side of the square, was built between 1892 and 1905 in a mix of Classical styles and northern Italian Renaissance. Bishop Absalon, the city's founder, appears on a gilded statue above the main doorway. The interior is also extravagantly finished. It may only be viewed as part of a guided tour (Monday to Friday 3pm, Saturday 10am).

Bishop Absalo

In the foyer (Monday to Friday 10am–4pm, Saturday 10am–1pm) stands **Jens Olsens Verdensur**, a unique timepiece with 12 works and 19,000 parts. The world clock's mechanisms, which have to be wound up once a week, give the exact time, date, time of sunrise and sunset and other data. It's possible to climb to the balcony of the 106-m (347-ft) tower and look down over the city centre and across the Øresund to Sweden (1 June to 30 September, Monday to Friday 10am, noon and 2pm, Saturday noon; otherwise Monday to Saturday at noon).

Jens Olsens Verdensur

To the right of City Hall steps, towards the busy H.C. Andersens Boulevard, it's easy to overlook a statue of the famous fairytale writer – he really deserves somewhere better. To the left of City Hall, on Vester Voldgade, stands a pillar with a statue of two **lur players**. Erected in 1914, this model of two Bronze Age musicians is much admired.

Now on to the fun side of this tour. One possible starting point is the American-style museum of curiosities just behind the *lur* players. **Ripley's Believe it or not!** (1 June to 31 August, daily 10am–10pm; otherwise Sunday to Friday 10am–6pm, Saturday 10am–8pm) is based on a venerable American newspaper strip and, if you're keen to learn more about the demise of aviation pioneers or are interested in how you can smoke with your eyes, this attraction will be of interest.

Situated in a small, Renaissance villa on the other side of City Hall Square, ★ **Louis Tussaud's Wax Museum** ❷ (1 May to 15 September, daily 10am–11pm; otherwise 10am–6pm) may have more appeal. Personalities from the worlds of politics, history, art and show business form the basis of this skilfully staged collection of wax celebrities, which is updated from time to time. Members of the Nordic royal families are also included among the exhibits, and those who can pluck up the courage should also see the Chamber of Horrors. Louis

The Wax Museum's royal residents

was a descendant of Madame Marie Tussaud, whose London museum became the model for waxworks throughout the world.

Housed in the same building is the ★ **Tivolimuseet** (1 May to 15 September, daily 11am–6pm; otherwise Tuesday to Sunday 10am–4pm). This three-storey building enables visitors to look behind the scenes at the way this extraordinary pleasure park has developed. Fairground stalls, rides, games machines, flea circus, festivals, firework displays, pantomimes, variety shows, concerts, the Tivoli Guard – there are so many themes to explore, all of which arouse the curiosity and sense of anticipation, even if some of the attractions haven't stood the test of time especially well. The use of modern media, such as a short film showing pyrotechnics experts preparing the traditional firework display, helps to overcome the museum's somewhat old-fashioned appearance.

However, even the most interesting museum is no substitute for the real thing. If you are in the museum and you can wait no longer, you can enter the park by a special entrance. Otherwise follow the H. C. Andersens Boulevard and Vesterbrogade for about 150m (160yds) to the **Main Entrance [A]** to the ★★★ **Tivoli Gardens** ❸ (1 May to 15 September, Sunday to Wednesday 11am–midnight, Thursday to Saturday 11am–1am; *see detailed map on page 18*).

16

Tivoli Gardens by day and night

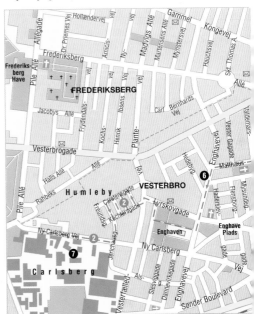

Neatly uniformed attendants welcome new arrivals. These men in their old-fashioned outfits embody the sense of tradition and dignity, the special qualities of the Tivoli which make it more than just a pleasure park. For proof of this, look to the left at the **Pantomime Theatre [B]**, whose actors portray characters from the Italian *commedia dell'arte*, such as Harlequin, Columbine and Pierrot. Their stories are not accompanied by tape recordings, but by a small orchestra, which then plays on between performances in the nearby **Pavilion [C]**.

Also close to the entrance is a second, larger **open-air stage [D]**, where various performers display their talents. On Wednesday and Saturday at 11.45pm, it is also the venue for the keenly awaited firework display. Following a tradition that goes back to the 19th century, the Tivoli Guard also meet here. This troupe consists of about 100 boys aged between 9 and 16, who, on certain days, parade through the park in red and white uniforms and bearskin caps, playing military music. Most of these youngsters are very keen and their enthusiasm compensates for their lack of musical experience.

Return to the circular path through the Tivoli and keep left towards H.C. Andersens Boulevard, past a small lake. At this point, it is worth investigating the park's history. The lake is the remains of a moat which surrounded the overcrowded town until 1856. The old western ramparts roughly followed the course of Vester Voldgade – hence

Pierrot in Pantomime and the Open-Air Stage

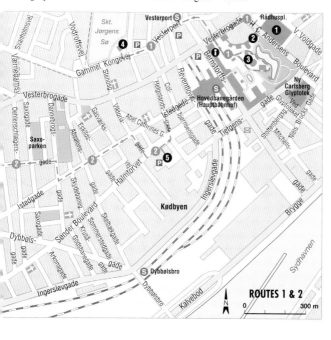

ROUTES 1 & 2

0   300 m

The pagoda

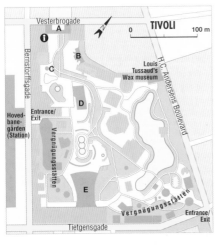

Park patrol

the name – and on the present City Hall Square stood **Vesterport** (the west gate), where customs duties were levied on goods arriving in the city.

Outside the Vesterport was the cattle market and a vast wood store. It was here in the mid-19th century that the railway station was built. With so much movement backwards and forwards through the area, it was almost predestined to become a public pleasure park.

The driving force behind the park was the polyglot entrepreneur, Georg Carstensen. He had travelled widely and seen the idea in practice in other cities. The successful formula was to be a mixture of a park, a venue for cultural events and a fair. First of all, he had to persuade the king, Christian VIII, of his plan's viability, as the earmarked land followed ramparts which belonged to the army. The Tivoli finally opened its gates on 15 August 1843. The first buildings were made of wood and canvas canopies so that, in the event of a military threat – the last had been in living memory between 1801 and 1814 (*see pages 10–11*) – they could be demolished quickly. One of the first attractions was a cable-car ride, a model of which can be seen in the Tivolimuseet (*see page 16*).

Over the years, the Tivoli has been modernised and greatly extended. The zigzag lines of the old ramparts have gradually disappeared and the surviving lake in the middle has become part of the park. The Pantomime Theatre was opened in 1871, the main entrance with its striking dome in 1890.

Carstensen, who died in 1857, is remembered by a bronze statue at the entrance. In 1944, as an act of reprisal, the Germans destroyed some of the Tivoli buildings but, within a few weeks the park was back in business, albeit on a temporary stage. Tivoli Gardens have survived a series of crises. Even when the accounts occasionally dived into the red, the attraction's future was never in serious doubt. Since 1843, some 500 million visitors have passed through the gates, and some 4 million guests now pay to enter it every year.

With its lake and lawns, water features and flowerbeds, the Tivoli fulfils its role as a traditional, landscaped garden but, as darkness falls, the atmosphere changes as thousands of electric lights come on to illuminate the scene. These, and the Chinese or Moorish-inspired buildings, create an exotic ambiance, and, in keeping with the Danes' love of life, have a cheering and relaxing effect.

More than 20 restaurants and cafés complete the picture. Many of these offer inexpensive lunches, although in the evenings prices can be much higher. Even so, on warm summer evenings it can be difficult getting a seat in such places as Grøften or Balkonen (*see page 80*). These restaurants are favourite meeting places for friends, families and business people. Some of them are situated by the park's perimeter and can be reached via their own entrance, an important consideration for those establishments which have live music performances, as they are then accessible when the Tivoli is closed. **Tivoli Jazzhouse** (*see page 83*) is a very popular venue for jazz fans, while Vise Vers Huset specialises in folk music and sing-along sessions.

A ringside seat

The main **Concert Hall [E]** also has a separate entrance, so that access is possible outside the summer season. Some 100 or so concerts are held here during the season with about half of them free of charge.

Most of the rides, fairground stalls and amusement arcades are concentrated along Tietgensgade. Among the most popular are the old-fashioned rollercoaster and the high-speed merry-go-rounds. Boat trips on the lake are also available. If a proper festival is taking place, then you can buy what is called a 'Tur-Pas', a bargain day ticket which can be used on about 25 different rides and other attractions.

19

Return to the main entrance. On the other side of Vesterbrogade lies **Axeltorv**, a square with plenty more amusement arcades. Just to the right stands **Scala**, a high-rise boutique complex (*see page 85*). It was built in the late 1980s on the site of the **Scala Teater**, a theatre which came to prominence in the inter-war years, when people flocked here to watch the reviews and forget their cares for a few

Bustle on Axeltorv

hours. The famous chanteuse Josephine Baker once trod the boards here in her unforgettable banana skirt. Now the Scala building only has bananas in the shop or on the menu, while the entertainment tradition is restricted to the cinema on the top floor.

The strikingly painted **Palads Teatret**, further up Axeltorv, can boast over 20 different screens. You can prepare yourself for the film by stocking up at the cinema's own sweet shop on the ground floor. The final stage of the Vesterport passes first the S-station of the same name and then the **Imperial**, Copenhagen's largest cinema. The polar bear logo belongs to the Nordisk Films Kompagni (*see page 76*). A little further along Gammel Kongevej lies **Skt Jørgens Lake**.

Inside the Planetarium

You simply cannot miss the ★ **Tycho Brahe Planetarium** ❹ (daily 10.30am–9pm) with its 36m (118ft) high, cylindrical tower and diagonal roof. For the best view of this striking building, cross to the other side of the lake and take a stroll along the promenade.

Inside the planetarium is a small exhibition on astronomy and space travel. The main draw, however, must be the film auditorium with its 23m (75ft) wide dome-shaped screen, and its *stjerneforestillinger* or 'star shows' are definitely worth sampling. Thanks to the latest computer technology, visitors can undertake a fascinating journey through space, encountering such phenomena as the Northern Lights, comets and supernovas.

The advertising for the Omnimax film performances takes up the same theme: higher, faster, wider, further. What is on offer are clips of free-climbers, rock stars and other successful people. There is also a restaurant serving Danish and international cuisine (Friday to Monday 10.30am–9pm, Tuesday to Thursday 9.45am–9pm).

The Tycho Brahe Planetarium

Route 2

Vesterbro – a quarter in the midst of change

Istedgade – Øksnehallen – Hedebygade Kareen – Enghaven – Humleby – Carlsberg Brewery *See map on
pages 16–17*

'There are more brothels, drug-addicts, gamblers and no-
hopers here than anywhere else in town,' a police inspector
told his colleagues in the detective film *Murder in the
Dark*. On reflection, perhaps Vesterbro was lucky to have
acquired this reputation, because it was spared the predatory advances of the speculators and the thoughtless building boom of the 1960s and '70s. But the decline of this
high-rise, working-class quarter, built at the turn of the
century, has been arrested. By 2007, some 5 billion krone
will have been spent giving the area a facelift. This five-
hour stroll through Vesterbro, possibly shortened with a
bus ride or two, explores the past and witnesses some of
the new developments. Throughout the quarter, major
building works are in progress.

21

The route starts at the central station. It could not be more
fitting: do not leave the central station via the main exit,
but by the rear entrance, which opens out onto the old red-
light boulevard, **Istedgade**, where sex is unashamedly sold
to foreigners. However, the neon lights are not quite so
plentiful as you might expect. Shops selling everyday
items, second-hand stores and pubs abound, too, and their
prices are considerably lower than in the fancy shoppers'
paradise by Strøget (*see page 32*). If you want to explore
the area, then take a detour off Istedgade. Helgolandsgade
leads straight to Halmtorvet, where the prostitutes wait for
custom during the day. The side wall of **Halmtorvet 3**
is an object lesson in the renovation business. Over the
next few years, the young shoots of climbing plants will
run rampant over the trellis. Covering walls with foliage
is one way of reducing noise; it also protects properties
from extreme temperatures and filters exhaust gases.

Beyond Halmtorvet lies an abandoned industrial area,
and then ★ **Øksnehallen** ❺ (Tuesday, Thursday and Friday noon–6pm, Wednesday noon–10pm, Saturday and
Sunday 10am–6pm). The preserved abattoir serves as a
symbol for the re-wakening of Vesterbro. Using reclaimed
building materials, the old building has been turned into
an ingenious new 4,000 sq.metre exhibition hall while
retaining much of the character and detail of the original
building. As well as temporary displays, a permanent exhibition in the building will eventually open to describe
Vesterbro's revival.

*Øksnehallen:
sculpture and interior*

Saxogade facades

Enghaven Park and sculpture

Today it is perhaps hard to imagine that the green **Saxopark** was once a row of bleak backyards and poorly-maintained multi-storey tenements, each one divided up into small, dark flats with toilets on the stairways. For many years that was how working people lived in large parts of Vesterbro. Up until the 1970s, Saxogade was one of the poorest districts in the city, but long before the current renovation work started, this northern section was tidied up.

Matthæusgade leads towards one of the most spectacular renovation schemes in the quarter. On the right-hand side of Enghavevej lies the **Hedebygade Kareen ❻**, a restoration project from which architects, builders, town planners and environmentalists hope to learn a lot. This huge, new scheme takes into account social as well as ecological factors. It is no luxury development for well-heeled investors and tax-dodgers. All the modernisation work will benefit the existing residents.

Features of the scheme include creepers to grow up some of the facades, solar panels fitted to the roof at points which receive full sun, conduits to direct rainwater into reservoirs which will meet some of the neighbourhood's water requirements, and 'green' kitchens fitted out using environmentally-friendly materials and energy-saving equipment. Also incorporated are 'forcing frames' attached to the facades to serve the dual purpose of horticulture and balcony.

The highlight of the complex is the spacious inner courtyard that is to act as a 'green lung' for the surrounding environment. Vegetable and herb gardens for the cooks, playgrounds for the children – anything is possible. A community hall, constructed mainly from recycled materials, will be built at the sunniest spot beneath an insulating mound of earth that will form a sun terrace in the summer and a toboggan run in the winter. South-facing panoramic windows will absorb light and heat energy, which will be stored in water tanks and then fed through pipes to heat floors and walls.

The work is being financed by the city council and is expected to take several years. Once Hedebygade is finished, tourists will surely want to come and admire the scheme, but, until then, it is worth a short detour to see how the project is progressing. The main entrance to the courtyard is situated between Hedebygade 9 and 11.

Enghaven Park (1928) is situated on the right of the busy Enghavevej. This is the last opportunity for a break on this tour and can be particularly rewarding if the roses are in flower. On the other side of Vesterfælledvej lies **Humleby**, truly a gem of a place. This little settlement comprises rows of houses, built between 1886 and 1891 to accommodate the Carlsberg brewery workers.

The cobbled Ny Carlsberg Vej crosses in front of the famous ★★ **Carlsberg brewery** ❼ premises (guided tours Monday to Friday 11am and 2pm), which straddle the districts of Vesterbro and Valby. To enter the works, which employs some 1,300 people, you will have to pass through a portal that is supported by four 5m (16ft) high Indian elephants. These sculptures, dating from 1901, are based on a design prepared by one of Copenhagen's most celebrated architects, Vilhelm Dahlerup. Beyond the portal, turn right towards the rather less striking main entrance. This is where the guided tours begin.

Carlsberg's elephants

The tour of the factory alternates between past and present. Its main sights include the historic, computer-controlled brewing hall, the modern fermenting and storage tanks, an abandoned bottling plant built at around the turn of the century and the present-day plant where a handful of workers keep an eye on the automated process from behind the machinery and conveyor belts. A bottle gallery displays examples of all the surviving types of Danish beer. The 20 strong Jutland horses that are lovingly cared for in the stables provide good publicity for the company. They are often seen on the city streets pulling brewery carts.

The brewery facade

Carlsberg brewery invest heavily in advertising and, to help create a positive image, at the conclusion of the guided tour, the company lays on a generous sampling session for its guests. The beer tasting takes place in an impressive hall decorated with statues. By now it should be clear that Carlsberg is no ordinary company.

The history of Carlsberg

Jacob Christian Jacobsen (1811–87) was not interested in simply taking over his father's small brewery. He had plans for a large, modern factory, but, before embarking on any rash schemes, he set about improving the basic product. In the mid-18th century Danish beer was a barely

Beer tasting in progress

A flavour to savour

tolerable brew, so Jacobsen toured Germany in search of the perfect beer and he returned from Bavaria with new yeast. Jacobsen now knew he could produce something very special. By 1847, a brand new brewery on a hill (Danish = *berg*) outside the ramparts was opened. The product was to be known as Carlsberg – Carl was the name of his son.

When Carl (1842–1914) grew up he joined the family firm, but differences soon emerged between father and son. In 1881, the dispute came to a head when Carl opened the 'Ny Carlsberg' (New Carslberg) brewery right next to his father's 'Gamle Carlsberg' (Old Carlsberg). The old man took his revenge by bequeathing his estate to the 'Carlsbergfond' foundation, which he had founded in 1876. This body was set up with the brewery profits to provide financial assistance to science and the arts. Carl Jacobsen also wanted to be remembered as a lover of culture and so he set up his own foundation, bequeathing his fortune to the similar 'Ny Carlsbergfond'. His first project was the construction of the 'Ny Carlsberg Glyptotek' in 1906 *(see Route 3, page 25)*.

The breweries and foundations have now been merged into one company, to which the Holmegaard glass factory, the Royal Copenhagen Porcelain Manufactory, Georg Jensen Silver and, since 1970, the Tuborg brewery also belong. Carlsberg and Tuborg beers are now brewed in 41 countries and on four continents and are drunk in more than 140 countries.

The Carlsberg foundation continues to support science and the arts – there is hardly a decent exhibition in the country that does not receive some money from it. Funds are administered from its headquarters in Dantes Plads opposite the Glyptotek.

Route 3

Art, culture and kings

Ny Carlsberg Glyptotek – Nationalmuseet – Slotshol-men – Christiansborg Palace – Royal Library Gar-den – Børsen – Holmens Kirke – Thorvaldsens Museum – Holmens Canal

This tour covers the city's main historic sights, starting with an extraordinary collection of art, funded from the sale of beer. It then goes straight to Denmark's oldest museum and on to Slotsholmen, where between the 12th and the 14th centuries Bishop Absalon's castle and the first royal palace were built. While it is true that the royal family no longer live on Slotsholmen, it remains an im-portant centre of power, where the Folketing – the Dan-ish parliament – still meets. It's possible to spend a day wandering around the museums, but you'll have to take a break for a snack at some time. Set out from City Hall Square in the direction of Tivoli Gardens.

Take H.C. Andersens Boulevard southwards to Dantes Plads. On its west side stands a striking, classical build-ing with a columned portal and domed roof, another work by the respected architect, Vilhelm Dahlerup. This is the ★★ **Ny Carlsberg Glyptotek** ❶ (Tuesday to Sunday 10am– 4pm; free admission on Wednesday and Sunday) – a museum of art financed by the Carlsberg brewery (*see opposite*). The company donates much of its profits to the arts and science.

Ny Carlsberg Glyptotek: winter garden

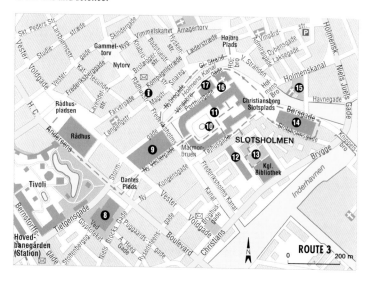

The Glyptotek possesses one of northern Europe's most valuable collections and, although the emphasis is on the Egyptian, Etruscan, Greek and Roman periods, the museum's founders, Carl Jacobsen, and his wife, Ottilia, were great lovers of French art and sculpture, so it has a large French section, where works by such famous artists as Cézanne, Gauguin and Rodin are on display.

Degas sculpture and Cézanne paintings

The Danish collection, which displays mainly 19th- and 20th-century works, also has a solid reputation. From an architectural point of view, the undoubted highlight is the delightful winter garden with its fountains and abundant greenery; there is also a fine new extension complete with glass-covered staircase.

Opposite the main entrance to the Glyptotek, Dantes Plads narrows to become Ny Vestergade. This labyrinthine building houses the ★★ **Nationalmuseet** **❾** (Tuesday to Sunday 10am–5pm), Denmark's largest museum. It occupies the whole of the block between Ny Vestergade, Vester Voldgade and Frederiksholms Canal. Built in the 1740s as a palace for the crown prince, it was later extended on several occasions. From 1845, items of artistic interest from the king's treasury were stored here and it soon developed into the national museum.

Nationalmuseet: the Sun Chariot of Trundholm

Three of the six huge sections focus on Danish history from the Stone Age to modern times. The largest section houses ethnographic exhibits from non-European countries. Of particular interest here is the Greenland exhibition with its portrayal of Eskimo life. Section 5 deals with the Classical era, its displays devoted to the Ancient Egyptians, the Middle East, Ancient Greece and the Roman Empire. The Royal Coin and Medal Collection has pieces from all over the world. In addition, the Frihedsmuseet (*see page 51*), the Open-Air Museum, which specialises in rural crafts, and the Bredemuseet, where cultural exhibitions are held (both in Lyngby) also form part of the Nationalmuseet.

Plan your time here carefully. To make the most of the museum, ask at the reception for a plan of the building and then choose the sections which interest you most. The atmosphere is rather austere, the attendants serious and ever-present and visitors are expected to behave in accordance with the classical surroundings. Only the chatter of children in school parties relieves the solemn mood. If you want to take a break for refreshments, make for the museum's highly regarded restaurant, but be prepared for equally exalted prices.

Art made easy in the children's section

Despite the museum's grandeur, children are welcome. In fact, there is an exhibition entitled 'Art made easy', in which youngsters of all ages can explore their creative talents.

26

Ny Vestergade leads on to the Frederiksholms Canal, where, just a few yards to the right, lies a popular *frokost* restaurant 'Kanal Cafeen' – an inexpensive alternative to the National Museum's restaurant. Culinary delights served beneath the fishing nets include *smørrebrød* with herring or eel, plaice or salmon.

Slotsholmen or Castle Island, the majestic centre of the city, extends to the east as far as the sound between Sealand and Amager and is itself enclosed by a semi-circular canal. The first buildings here were constructed on thousands of tree trunks. Ny Vestergade opens on to the **Marmorbroen** (Marble Bridge). This rococo-style structure was built between 1741 and 1745 under the direction of Nicolai Eigtved, who was working on the crown prince's palace at the same time. The bridge was restored in 1996, together with the two guard rooms which flank the entrance to Slotsholmen.

Under the marble bridge

Behind the bridge lies the enormous, oval riding ground, the **Ridebanen** ❿ (1 May to 30 September, Friday to Sunday 2–4pm; otherwise Saturday and Sunday only 2–4pm), where the horses from the royal stables are regularly trained. On weekday mornings, as long as the weather is fine, there is a good chance that visitors will be able to watch the horses practising. The stables in the block to the right, which also accommodate the royal coaches, saddles and harnesses, can be seen outside the equine working day.

Only a few yards away in the same block lies the old court theatre. From 1767 to 1881 it was a stage for opera and drama; now it is the **Teatermuseet** (Wednesday 2–4pm, Saturday and Sunday noon–4pm) and visitors can inspect the auditorium, the boxes, the stage, the changing rooms and the props.

The Ridebanen

Statue of Christian IX

Underground remains of Absalon's castle

Firepower at the Arsenal Museum

At the end of the riding ground, bear to the left and pass the **Equestrian Statue of Christian IX** in front of ★ **Christiansborg Palace ⓫**. Its dark granite facade, like many of the other buildings on Slotsholmen, creates a rather gloomy and melancholy impression. Small wonder then that the royal family prefers to live in Amalienborg Palace. In fact, few quiet outdoor retreats exist anywhere on Slotsholmen. The Danish parliament, the **Folketing**, works in the right-hand (eastern) and central (northern) blocks.

It is the proximity of the country's political base that requires the Queen to stay in Christiansborg. In accordance with established protocol, she invites guests to the **Royal Reception Chambers**. Meetings with foreign ambassadors take place in the Audience Room, while guests of the State dine in the Red Hall. If these rooms are not in use, they are open to the public during the day. Guided tours are available in English.

Pass through the large doorway in the north wing and descend into historic Christiansborg. There were four earlier palaces, starting with the castle of Bishop Absalon, said to be the city's founder. This was extended and converted on several occasions (1137–1369). When **Slot København** no longer met the requirements of the absolutist monarchs, it was demolished (1731–32). The two later palaces, which bore the Christiansborg name, both fell victim to fires (1794 and 1884).

When in 1906 excavation work was taking place for the present palace, workmen stumbled across foundations for walls, towers, fountains and water pipes, which were part of **Absalon's castle**. These finds have been preserved in the palace cellar and can be viewed alongside photographs of the excavation work (1 May to 30 September, daily 9.30am–3.30pm; otherwise Tuesday, Thursday and Saturday 9.30am–3.30pm).

The Folketing occupies more than 320 rooms in Christiansborg. Public entry to the parliament building is not through the inner courtyard, but at the other end of the east wing. At the bottom of the staircase, a sign indicates whether and when conducted tours of the Folketing are taking place.

Access to the Royal Library is through a gate opposite the staircase. On the right, Tøjhusgade leads back to the Frederiksholms Canal, which passes the **Tøjhusmuseet ⓬** or Arsenal Museum (Tuesday to Saturday noon–4pm). This 400-year-old, 163m (530ft) long brick building houses a collection of weaponry ranging from daggers to cannons to Hawk missiles. Little is said about the background to the wars or their victims, and the museum is nothing more than a military parade of weapons of destruction.

The **Royal Library Garden** is Slotsholmen's 'green lung'. It is a carefully-tended area with a lawn that, unlike other parks in Copenhagen, is off limits to visitors. Near the pond, a statue recalls the philosopher Søren Kierkegaard.

The Royal Library Garden

Det Kongelige Bibliotek (Monday to Saturday 9am–7pm) has existed since Frederik III's regency. It is now home to some 2½ million books and 55,000 manuscripts, including those written by Kierkegaard, Hans Christian Andersen and Karen Blixen. As there is no longer room for every new publication, an extension is being built by the banks of the canal. During the first half of the 16th century, the water extended right up to the present garden and there was even a landing stage. You can see one of the mooring rings on the wall. In 1867–68 the area was filled in and by 1906 the library and garden were completed. The library foyer is now used for temporary exhibitions.

The Reading Room

Return via the Folketing forecourt and then take two right turns. In front stands what is probably the most impressive edifice on Slotsholmen, the ★ **Børsen** or Stock Exchange. Today, it can only be viewed from outside, but it was originally a warehouse in Dutch Renaissance style, dating from the early 17th century.

The Stock Exchange

For King Christian IV, a great lover of pomp and splendour, the elongated, two-storey building was not grand enough, so in 1625 he commissioned the first of 18 striking gables and the 54m (177ft) high spire – the latter is actually made up of four entwined dragons' tails. The three golden crowns on top represent Denmark, Norway and Sweden. In the middle of the 19th century, the currency and security dealers moved into the building, hence its name. Although these traders have since found a new home, the interior of the old stock exchange is still used as offices. The ornamentation and sculptures on the facade

and the doorway reveal that it is some time since the building was last restored. Until recently the public was allowed inside once a year in September when it hosted a large antiques exhibition.

On the other side of the street and **Holmens Canal**, the tower of ★ **Holmens Kirke** ⓯ (15 May to 15 September, Monday to Friday 9am–2pm, Saturday 9am–noon; otherwise Monday to Saturday 9am–noon) points skyward. The church was built originally as a smithy for making anchors, but in 1619, on the orders of Christian IV, it was turned into a church for mariners' families. Two of Denmark's maritime heroes, Niels Juel (1629–97) and Peter Tordenskjold (1690–1720), who both achieved several victories over the Swedish fleet, are buried here, but ordinary seamen who lost their lives in the two world wars are also remembered.

Because of its isolated position, it survived earlier fires and has retained its original baroque pulpit and altar, an unusual achievement for a Copenhagen church. One particularly interesting piece is the 1.2m (3ft 9in) high font, dating from 1646, which bears the initials of Christian IV. It is said that it was used to baptise African slaves.

Slotsholmen has its own church. To get there, cross the **Christiansborg Palace Square** with its equestrian statue of Frederik VII. The inscription translates as 'The love of the people is my strength'.

Christiansborg Slotskirke ⓰ stands at the point where the river bends sharply. It dates from around the same time as the second Christiansborg. It managed to withstand the destructive fire of 1884, but not an emergency flare that went off course in 1992. The roofing timbers caught fire and the copper dome collapsed. Fortunately, most of the precious fittings were saved and the church was restored to its former splendour.

Holmens Canal views

Cross **Prins Jørgens Gård** to reach the ★ **Thorvaldsens Museum** ⑰ (Tuesday to Sunday 10am–5pm; admission free). Bertel Thorvaldsen (*see page 73*) is regarded as one of Denmark's greatest classical sculptors. At the age of 11, the young Bertel was accepted by the Copenhagen Art Academy. He then lived for more than 40 years in Rome, receiving commissions from the Vatican and many European kings and princes, who appreciated the aesthetic ideals of antiquity. He returned to Copenhagen in 1838 and was appointed an honorary citizen. On his death, he bequeathed his works, his own collection and his estate to the nation on the condition that a museum was built for the artistic treasures. His plans, castings, originals and replicas, plus his antiques and collection of paintings, are all on display here.

Thorvaldsens Museum: Ganymede statue

It's worth taking a stroll around the outside of the museum to admire the life-size frieze, which was designed under the supervision of the respected architect M.G. Bindebøll. It shows Thorvaldsen's triumphant return to Copenhagen and the arrival of his sculptures at the museum. The master himself is buried in the museum's inner courtyard.

31

Both the Slotskirke and Thorvaldsens Museum are situated by Vindebrogade and the **Holmens Canal**. If you cross to the other side and walk back along Nybrogade, you will pass a row of art galleries, antique shops and restaurants. The brick building on the corner of Nybrogade and Naboløs is the Ministry of Culture.

Nybrogade becomes **Gammel Strand** ('Old Beach'). This refers to the time before any houses or palaces were built on Slotsholmen and the waters of the Øresund extended this far up. Until the 1950s, it was the site of the fish market. Only one or two of the market stalls remain, catering primarily for the tourist trade. A statue on the **Højbro** bridge recalls the 'fishwives' who were once key figures in the everyday life of the district. One part of Copenhagen life that has survived is the famous 'Krogs Fiskerestaurant' (*see page 80*). Enjoy one of its fine fish dishes, after an exhilarating cruise in one of the sightseeing boats which leave from Gammel Strand. In the basement at Gammel Strand 48, Copenhagen's first photo gallery was opened during 1996. However, the rooms which house the **Fotografisk Center** (Tuesday to Sunday, 10am–5pm) are scarcely big enough to meet demand.

Højbro Plads

The redesigned, traffic-calmed **Højbro Plads** is the setting for a modest market. Bishop Absalon, the city's founder, surveys the Højbro from his horse. Højbro Plads serves as the link between the busy Strøget shopping street and central Amagertorv. After the calm of Slotsholmen, the hive of activity in the commercial heart of the city comes as quite a shock to the system.

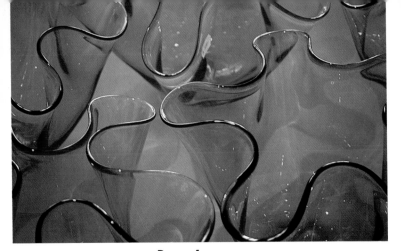

Exquisite glass

Route 4

Shops and museums

Amagertorv – Museum Erotica – Gråbrødretorv – Skindergade – Rundetårn – Filmhuset – Arbejdermuseet – Botanical Gardens – Geologisk Museum – Statens Museum for Kunst *See map on page 35*

In many circles, the mere mention of the word 'erotic' is greeted with a stony silence. Some may regard erotic films as good entertainment, but few would class them as art and even fewer would be interested in the history of the genre. Attitudes are different in Copenhagen.

Start this tour at Amagertorv. Take a stroll past the tempting shops in Strøget and end with a wander through the parks and gardens to the north of the city centre.

Amagertorv, part of the Strøget

Amagertorv, which tapers off from east to west, near Gammel Strand, was an important marketplace in the city's early days. Now, it is just a small part of the busy 1.8km (over a mile) long pedestrianised **Strøget**, Denmark's top shopping street. Amid the hustle and bustle of shoppers, it is easy to overlook the delightful **Storkespringvandet** or Stork Fountain (1894). If you look closer, you will see that the three birds resemble herons rather than storks. From an architectural point of view, the centrepiece of the square is the Dutch Renaissance-style No. 6, which dates from 1616 and so ranks as one of the city's oldest buildings. It is now used by one of Denmark's most prestigious companies, Royal Copenhagen, as a showroom for their chinaware, and is flanked by two illustrious neighbours: the silversmith 'Georg Jensen' to the right and the modern design store 'Illums Bolighus' to the left.

The Stork Fountain

As you would imagine, **Royal Copenhagen** has something to do with the Danish monarchy. When the porcelain factory was founded in 1775, the royal family were majority shareholders. Later on, they took it over completely, but now Royal Copenhagen is an independent company and part of the Carlsberg empire. The factory, situated in Frederiksberg (*see Route 8, page 60*), is renowned for its large porcelain pieces and underglaze painting. A tour round the factory is a fascinating experience and also provides the chance to buy a classy souvenir or some good value seconds. The city centre **showroom** (Monday to Thursday 10am–6pm, Friday 10am–7pm, Saturday 10am–2pm; in addition from 1 May to 30 September, Saturday 10am–5pm, Sunday noon–5pm; admission free) sells china sets and individual pieces, including the 'Blue Fluted' and 'Flora Danica' designs – all hand-painted, some requiring thousands of brushstrokes. Although the porcelain is usually of a traditional design, the glassware comes in modern shapes and colours, both as ornamental pieces and functional objects.

Royal Copenhagen: proud associations

The silverware shop, **Georg Jensen** (No.4), exemplifies fine craftmanship. Since it was founded in 1904, the company has had two specialisms: cutlery and tableware, on the one hand, and jewellery, on the other. Georg Jensen was both a trained silversmith and a sculptor. When he died in 1935, the *New York Times* described him as one of the finest silver designers of the last 300 years. Part of his company's reputation, however, is derived from his reliance on creative, contemporary artists. These craftsmen were skilled in manipulating not just silver, but other materials such as steel – and this proved very useful during the years when the price of silver was prohibitive. The finest of Jensen's products can be admired in the showroom and the adjoining **Georg Jensen Museum**. For opening times, see Royal Copenhagen (*above*).

Georg Jensen for silverware

The **Illums Bolighus** (No. 10) furniture store (Monday to Thursday 10am–6pm, Friday 10am–7pm, Saturday 10am–2pm; in addition from 1 May to 30 September, Saturday 10am–5pm and Sunday 10am–noon) contains countless other examples of excellent Danish design, although potential buyers will need to go armed with a bulging wallet. A wander through the open, panelled galleries is definitely worthwhile, even if you have no intention of buying.

Illums Bolighus for furniture

Opposite these high-class stores lies a property dedicated to that dying breed, the smoker. **WO Larsen**, at No. 9 since 1864, has a fine selection of pipes on offer, but the small **tobacco museum** (Monday to Wednesday 10am–6pm, Thursday 10am–7pm, Friday 10am–5pm) in the basement may prove more interesting. Smoking paraphernalia from all over the world is on display here.

Inside Illum

The top floor of **Illum** department store is the perfect place for a rest and refreshment, but you may well get sidetracked by the superb range of goods on sale on the way there. As well as a cafeteria, it also boasts a pasta and pizza restaurant and a bistro with a high-class menu. The abundant display of plants, the glass ceiling, plus the stage and piano, create a warm and inviting atmosphere.

Købmagergade is another busy, traffic-free shopping street. The name derives from the *kjødmager* – the butchers – who settled in this part of the city during the 15th century. It is worth knowing where the post office is (No. 33) but otherwise, there are few buildings of interest.

Copenhagen, with its liberally-minded populace, is one of the few places in Europe that would tolerate a ★ **Museum Erotica** ⑱ (1 May to 30 September, daily 10am–11pm; otherwise Monday to Friday and Sunday 11am–8pm, Saturday 10am–9pm). But it is not simply a display of naked bodies. The management has sought to discriminate between love, sex and commercial pornography. So, as long as the word 'sex' doesn't cause undue embarrassment, you'll probably enjoy seeing how eroticism and sexuality have been expressed since the time of the ancient Greeks.

However, not every visitor responds equably to the bare facts as displayed here and some tourists have been known to beat a hasty retreat when they realise what they have let themselves in for.

Refreshment on Gråbrødretorv

A shortcut through Løvstræde leads to **Gråbrødretorv**. This delightful square with a huge beech tree has been spared from traffic for many years and that partly explains the reason for its numerous pubs and restaurants. When the sun shines, customers quickly spill out onto the pavement. Gråbrødretorv owes its name, the 'market of the Grey Brothers', to the Franciscan monastic order. The monks, known locally as the 'Grey Brothers', had a monastery here from 1238 to 1530. All the nearby buildings were destroyed in the Great Fire of 1728 apart from the vaults of the abandoned monastery. Today, the 'Peder Oxe', a favourite restaurant with Copenhageners (*see page 80*), occupies the site above the cellar (No. 11). The compact row of houses (Nos. 1–11) is typical of the buildings that appeared after the Great Fire – proper wall instead of half-timber, three to four floors, a mansard roof projecting as a gable. A fountain in the square was donated to the city when it celebrated its 800th birthday in 1967.

If you like shopping you can take a short detour to **Fiolstræde**, west of the square. There are a number of interesting antiques shops. Towards the northwest, Gråbrødretorv opens onto **Skindergade**, which then leads back

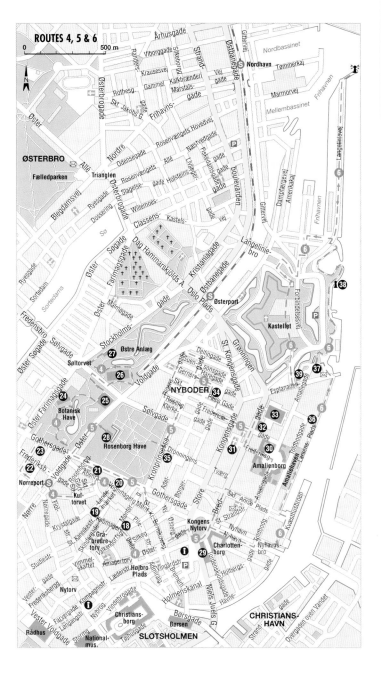

Rundetårn and its ramp

to Købmagergade. Some of the fine **half-timbered houses** in Skindergade have survived both fires and property speculators. Number 11 in red and – if you go through the gate – the pretty yellow house in the rear courtyard at No. 8, both date from the first half of the 18th century.

Back in Købmagergade, you will find yourself at the foot of the ★ **Rundetårn** ⓳ (1 June to 31 August, Monday to Saturday 10am–8pm, Sunday noon–8pm; otherwise Monday to Saturday 10am–5pm, Sunday noon–5pm. Observatory: 1 October to 15 March, Tuesday and Wednesday 7–10pm). Christian IV had the round tower built in 1642 as an observatory. Royalty and other dignitaries reached the top via a winding ramp 209m (685ft) long and wide enough for a carriage. The view from the 36m (118ft) tower takes in the whole of the city – but the Vor Frelsers Kirke offers an even better panorama (*see Route 7, page 55*). The observatory is open during the winter.

It is only a few yards across Landemærket to the **Filmhuset** ⓴, the home of the national film institutions: the **Danish Film Institute**, the **National Film Headquarters** and the **Danish Film Museum** (performances: Tuesday to Friday noon– 9.30pm, Saturday and Sunday 10am–9.30pm). Not many people are aware that, in the years before World War I, Denmark was one of the world's leading cinematographic nations (*see Culture, page 76*), so it is all the more interesting to delve into the history of Danish films via film performances that take place here (many of them with English subtitles).

Opposite the 'film house', on the corner of Gothersgade (No. 87), stands 'Kongens Kælder', a *frokost* restaurant. You may be tempted by a delicious *smørrebrød*, but it is open only on weekdays from 11am–4pm. (*See page 80.*)

From the cinema to music. Situated in narrow Åbenrå, the **Musikhistorisk Museum** ㉑ (1 May to 30 September, Friday to Wednesday 1–3.30pm; otherwise Saturday to Monday and Wednesday 1–3.30pm) is a source of fascination to anyone who loves music. In particular, its collection of instruments from the past 1,000 years steal the show. Occasionally, the History of Music Museum stages classical concerts, often using some of the ancient instruments normally kept for display. Ask at the entrance for details of any forthcoming events.

Hausergade connects Åbenrå with the traffic-calmed **Kultorvet**, a popular meeting-place for young people. The 'Café Klaptræet' (*see page 81*) is symbolic of the crisis that beset the Danish film industry earlier this century, when it had to contend first with the confusion of World War I and later with the emigration of film stars to America. Originally a café and cinema, only the furniture, posters and film rolls recall the glory days of the former cinema round the corner.

It's worth making a brief stop outside No. 9 in **Rosengården** to admire the small plaque. This portrayal of the Danish philosopher Søren Kierkegaard was the work of the caricaturist, Christian Klæstrup (1820–82), who once lived here. He was Denmark's first cartoonist and he had to put up with humourless censors who viewed all his drawings as an attack on the authorities.

Follow **Fiolstræde**, Copenhagen's third shopping street, for a short distance to the underground S-station of Nørreport on the main Nørre Voldgade. There is a turn-of-the-last-century **telephone kiosk** at the junction which until recently was used as a box office for concert tickets.

On the other side of Nørre Voldgade, which follows the course of the old ramparts, Vendersgade cuts through to **Israel Plads** ㉒ and Rømersgade. This square was so named in 1968 to recall the 25th anniversary of the German persecution of Danish Jews during World War II. The red stone beside Rømersgade was presented by the Israeli government in 1975.

37

From Monday to Saturday, fruit and vegetable stalls occupy the northern side of the square along Frederiksborggade. On Saturday during the summer months, the produce sellers are joined by a flea market. What is offered for sale here, however, would probably be best described as *bric-a-brac* rather than antiques (*see page 85*).

Historical museums usually focus on the great and the good. The Workers' Museum or **★★ Arbejdermuseet** ㉓ at Rømersgade No.22 (1879) tells a different story – and in a livelier and more informative way than is normal (1 July to 31 October, daily 10am–4pm; otherwise Tuesday to Sunday 10am–4pm). Many socialist heroes, such as

The Arbejdermuseet and exhibits

Wilhelm Liebknecht, August Bebel, Rosa Luxembourg and Clara Zetkin, spoke at public meetings in the large room at the back. It was, therefore, the ideal place for a museum dedicated to the class struggle.

The exhibitions begin in 1870 at a time when many workers were being exploited by industrialisation, when workers' leaders found themselves in prison and the police spied on meetings. Life was harsh and the conditions in the factories bleak. One of the most impressive displays traces the Sørensen family through three generations, mainly in the years before World War II. It shows how impoverished farmers and farmworkers arrived in the towns full of hope, how the world economic crisis affected everyday life, how working conditions changed in the various professions and the improvements that had to be won through struggle.

The 1950s were characterised by an improving social security safety net and greater purchasing power, but men and women still did not receive equal pay and there was a shortage of decent homes. It was during this period that canteens opened to provide cheap cakes and drinks for working people. The 'Café & Ølhalle 1892' *(see page 81)* situated in the museum serves traditional Danish fare.

Café & Ølhalle 1892

Israel Plads and Rømersgade have developed on the site of the old ramparts, as have the green areas to the north and south.

The ★ **Botanical Gardens**, just to the north of Gothersgade, is a delightful environment for a relaxing stroll (gardens: 1 May to 30 September, daily 8.30am– 6pm; otherwise 8.30am–4pm; conservatory: daily 10am– 3pm; other greenhouses: Saturday and Sunday 1–3pm. Admission free). Some 10 hectares (25 acres) of land contain a variety of plant life, including herbs, shrubs and rock gardens. Many of the plants are native to northern Europe, but some come from further afield.

Aspects of the Botanical Gardens

The impressive **conservatory ㉔**, opened in 1874 with the rest of the Botanisk Have, contains a marvellous collection of tropical and sub-tropical flora. There is a café just behind the conservatory, which serves refreshments during the summer.

The benches around the ponds are always very popular, but the Botanical Gardens cannot really compete with Rosenborg Have or Frederiksberg Have, as here the public are obliged to keep off the lawns. The small **Botanisk Museum** is only opened for special exhibitions.

A Renaissance building in the Botanical Gardens houses the **Geologisk Museum ㉕** (Tuesday to Sunday 1–4pm; admission free), a treasure trove of curiosities, which will be of interest to the layperson. The meticulously arranged mineral collection, the meteorites and the re-

cently-opened Greenland exhibition are the main focal points. It's not possible to enter the museum from the Botanical Gardens.

Statens Museum for Kunst: interior...

To the north of the wide Sølvgade, this green belt continues with the Østre Anlæg. This quiet, unassuming park provides the right setting for two art museums.

39

One grand building dating from 1896 houses the extremely worthwhile ★★ **Statens Museum for Kunst** ㉖ (Tuesday to Sunday 10am–5pm, Wednesday until 8pm). Any resemblance to the Ny Carlsberg Glyptotek is not a coincidence – the design originates from the same drawing board, that of Vilhelm Dahlerup. Visitors are always impressed by the small sculpture garden just in front of the Roman-style triumphal arch and flight of steps. A new extension towards the park has doubled the exhibition area.

Inside, the fine collection of European art dates from around 1530. The main themes are Danish painting, French 19th-century painting and modern art. Exhibitions are held here too. A collection of copperplate engravings and drawings, as well as montages by children, are also particularly interesting.

...and exterior

If you have still not seen enough fine art, then make your way to the second temple of culture in Østre Anlæg. **Den Hirschsprungske Samling** ㉗ (Wednesday 11am–9pm, Thursday to Monday 11am–4pm) focuses almost entirely on Danish art with a preference for 19th-century and early 20th-century painting. The collection owes its survival to the tobacco magnate, Heinrich Hirschsprung (1836–1908), who donated it to the state in 1902. It is interesting to ponder that a large part of the country's cultural heritage is accessible to the Danish nation only thanks to the benevolence of two individuals: one who made his fortune out of beer (*see Route 2, page 25*) and one who made it out of tobacco.

Route 5

The marching route of the Royal Life Guard

Rosenborg Castle – Rosenborg Have – Kongens Nytorv – Frederiksstaden – Amalienborg Palace – Marble Church – St Ansgar Cathedral – Kunstindustrimuseet – Nyboder – Davids Samling *See map on page 35*

Rosenborg Slot

Every day at 11.30am the Royal Life Guard marches from its base near Rosenborg Castle through the city centre to arrive at Amalienborg Palace for the changing of the guard ceremony exactly half-an-hour later. If the queen is in residence, the grand ceremony is carried out to musical accompaniment. While the soldiers with their thick bearskins may not be allowed to break their journey for a delicious snack or stand and stare admiringly at historic buildings, you can. To the north-west of Amalienborg lies the modest, but attractive Nyboder residential area.

Allow about four to five hours for this tour. To reach the starting point at Rosenborg Castle, you will need to take the S-train from City Hall Square to Nørreport or bus numbers 14, 16, 31, 42 or 43.

Christian IV loved grand festivals and splendour, so the medieval, rather gloomy Copenhagen Castle had little appeal for him. He ran the affairs of state from Frederiksborg Castle some 35km (22 miles) to the north-west of Copenhagen (*see pages 69–70*), but he really wanted a suitable residence in Copenhagen, so in 1605 he ordered work to start on a palace just outside the city walls. It was 1624, after several alterations and enlargements, before he declared himself content with the outcome: ★★ **Rosenborg Slot ㉓** (1 June to 31 August, daily 10am–

4pm; May and 1 September to 31 October, daily 11am–3pm; otherwise Tuesday, Friday and Sunday 11am–2pm). Christian had commissioned highly-regarded architects from the Netherlands and their work was a masterpiece of Dutch Renaissance. Constructed from red bricks, the facade was decorated with light sandstone. It was secured by a moat with drawbridge and surrounded by a magnificent rose garden, hence the name.

But no monarch ever resided permanently at Rosenborg. In 1722, less than 100 years after the castle was built, it was replaced as second residence by Fredensborg Slot near the delightful lake known as Esrum Sø. Rosenborg was more or less abandoned to become the 'royal family's store-room'. All the state treasures were brought here, as there was either no use or no space for them in the inhabited residences.

A palace packed with treasures

Consequently, the rooms in Rosenborg were splendidly furnished. They were opened up to the public in 1838 and they attract thousands of visitors every year. It is certainly worth obtaining the guidebook, which lists all the relics on display in the Marble Apartment, the Glass Chamber, the Knights' Hall, Bronze Chamber, etc. Finally, the Danish Crown Jewels wait patiently behind glass for their next outing.

41

The Crown Jewels

The Royal Life Guard, whose barracks are situated next door, patrols outside the castle. **Livsgardens Historiske Samling** (1 May to 30 September Tuesday and Sunday 11am–3pm, otherwise Sunday 11am–3pm; admission free) documents the history of the Royal Life Guard since it was founded in 1658.

The barracks

Every morning, the changing of the guard is rehearsed on the exercise ground at the site of the barracks. Those sightseers who wish to accompany the guards as they make their way through the city start to congregate outside the gates at around 11am. As the troops emerge in formation, a frantic scene ensues as tourists, often not too sure of the route the soldiers will take, hurry ahead with their cameras and videos in the hope of a good shot. The troops march past them and the whole episode starts again. Although they disregard the antics of the eager tourists, the guardsmen are not exempt from the routines of city life – they have to stop at red traffic lights.

If the queen is in residence, then the soldiers and band take the long route via Gothersgade, Nørre Voldgade, Frederiksborggade, Købmagergade, Østergade, Kongens Nytorv, Bredgade, Sankt Annæ Plads and Amaliegade. Otherwise, the shorter tour without musical accompaniment follows Gothersgade, Christian IX's Gade, Gammel Mønt, Kr. Bernikows Gade and Østergade to Kongens Nytorv.

The Bang & Olufsen showroom

The Royal Theatre

Magasin du Nord

★★ Rosenborg Have lies beside Gothersgade. This park, sometimes known as **Kongens Have** (or King's Garden) was laid out when Rosenborg Castle was built. Converted into an English-style garden in 1820, with its tall, old trees, statues, grassy lawns and shady walks, it is now an important 'breathing space' in the densely populated city. On a fine day, children from nearby kindergartens scramble on the playgrounds, weary legs rest on the park benches and tired minds enjoy a nap on the grass, but guards whose job it is to protect the nearby Crown Jewels still keep an eye on passers-by.

Follow **Østergade** at the northern end of Strøget for a short distance. The **Pistolstræde** passage on the left-hand side leads off on a short detour to cafés, restaurants and shops, where prices are comparable with those on Strøget. Just before the end of Østergade stands the **Bang & Olufsen** showroom. Step inside for the ultimate in hi-fi design. Strøget and Østergade emerge onto a huge and historic square: **Kongens Nytorv**. Its origins date from the end of the 17th century, when Christian IV (1670–87) was looking to expand the city northwards. His grandson, Christian V, had something grander in mind, namely a large, central square surrounded by stately buildings, which would fulfil Denmark's absolutist rulers' desire for splendour and panache.

The oldest, surviving building, **Charlottenborg Castle** (1672–83; *see page 48*) looks out towards the Sound. Others have been altered or replaced by more modern edifices, such as the **Royal Theatre** ㉙, a neo-Renaissance building dating from 1874. Two of Denmark's most celebrated writers, Adam Oehlenschlæger and Ludvig Holberg, stand by the steps to welcome arrivals. Two more fine facades flank the start of Strøget: on the left is the mega-department store **Magasin du Nord** (1894; *see page 85*), on the right the **Hotel d'Angleterre** (1874; *see page 94*), Denmark's top hotel.

The weight of traffic detracts somewhat from Kongens Nytorv's grandeur – it is the second-largest bus terminus after City Hall Square – even more so now that the plane trees that once grew in the central part of the square have had to give way to yet more cars. The equestrian statue there shows Christian V. Cast in lead in 1688, the monarch's weight caused irreparable damage to the horse, so in 1946 a new bronze statue was made to replace the original.

At the point where Bredgade joins Kongens Nytorv, the **Ravhuset** studio and shop (1 May to 30 September 10am–8pm; otherwise 10am–6pm) tempts tourists with its large collection of amber. Retrieving and processing amber is a traditional industry in Jutland and the translucent fossil resin has become a popular Danish souvenir and jewellery item.

Bredgade marks the gateway to **Frederiksstaden**, probably the most ambitious building project since the Middle Ages. In 1749, to the north-east of Kongens Nytorv, a district emerged where the nobility and the well-to-do middle classes could distance themselves from the rest of the city's residents. Their stately homes lined streets laid out in a regular pattern, in contrast to the winding streets of medieval Copenhagen. Court architect, Nicolai Eigtved was responsible for the ground-plan, of which Bredgade forms a part. The city's establishment has retained its preference for this quarter. Advertising agencies, solicitors and other offices vie for an address in **Palægade** and **Sankt Annæ Passage** (between Bredgade and Store Kongensgade), while the district's cafés, restaurants and boutiques compete equally strenuously for these wealthy professionals' custom.

The short route of the Royal Life Guard follows Bredgade as far as Frederiksgade; the longer march crosses **Sankt Annæ Plads** and then bears left into **Amaliegade**. A major attraction of this quiet street with its classical and baroque facades is the tastefully decorated 'Amalie' *frokost* restaurant at Amaliegade 11 (Monday to Friday 11.30am–4pm, Thursday and Friday also 6pm–midnight).

Just beyond the colonnade, the guardsmen reach their destination: ★ **Amalienborg Palace**. The octagonal square, overlooked by four ornate rococo palaces – initially occupied by four aristocratic families – was always intended to be the centrepiece of Frederiksstaden. When the second Christiansborg Palace burnt down in 1794, Christian VII moved his residence to Amalienborg. The colonnade was to link Christian VII's palace (to the right of the palace square) with that of the Crown Prince (on the left), where Margarethe II now lives. Traditionally, the royal family's rooms have been shared out among several palaces.

Amalienborg Palace

43

An evening view of one of the wings

The Royal Guard

Housed in the northern building, the small **Palace Museum ③⓪** (Kong Christians VIII's Palace: open 1 May to 20 October, daily 11am– 4pm; otherwise Tuesday to Sunday 11am–4pm) contains the private chambers and studies of kings Christian IX (1863–1906), Frederik VIII (1906–12) and Christian X (1912–47). The furnishings are a mixture of originals and reconstructions.

National flag

A visit to Amalienborg Palace should be timed to include the daily ★★ **Changing of the Guard** at noon. If the flag is flying, then the queen is in residence and the full Changing of the Guard ceremony will take place. Precise footsteps, manoeuvres and spoken commands ensure that the event goes off smoothly. When the officer in charge of the new company has received the order from his predecessor, 10 soldiers replace their counterparts at the palace entrances, while the rest disappear through a gate into the interior of the castle. Every two hours, the guards change duties. Finally, the original contingent set off back to their barracks along Frederiksgade, Store Kongensgade and Gothersgade. Spectators may only take photographs of the ceremony from specified places, although after the official handover there is little to see. In any case, attendants are on hand to ensure that the rules are followed. People whose behaviour is deemed to be too casual, perhaps if they sit down on the pavement or steps, will be approached and reprimanded. The area around the equestrian statue in the centre of the square is normally out of bounds. Sitting astride the horse is the man who lent his name to Frederiksstaden, Frederik V. The sculptor, J.F. Saly, took 20 years to complete the statue, which is highly regarded by the cognoscenti. The statue was completely renovated in 1998.

Frederik V on horseback

If you are standing in the middle of the palace square and cannot decide which road you should take, you will

almost certainly be drawn by the huge, copper dome of the ★ **Marble Church** ❸❶ (Monday, Tuesday, Thursday and Friday 11am–2pm, Saturday 11am–4pm, Sunday noon–4pm, Wednesday 11am– 6pm; admission free. Dome: 1 June to 31 August, Monday to Friday 11am and 12.45pm; otherwise Saturday 11am and Sunday noon). The church's proper name is **Frederiks Kirke**. Frederik V had in mind a splendid rococo church for Frederiksstaden and in 1749 imported vast quantities of marble from Norway. But even a royal contractor can run out of money and work slowed down. In 1770, four years after the king's death, the project was cancelled.

The partially completed building was left to decay for more than 100 years, but in 1874 the industrialist Tietgen financed the completion of the project. He retained the completed marble base and put most of his money into other extravagant features. Above the portal, 16 zinc statues represent important personalities in Danish church history, while the Italian Baroque dome is modelled on St Peter's in Rome. The dome, which can be viewed close-up from a gallery, dominates the interior too. Particularly striking features include the royal box and the paintings, which depict the 12 apostles.

The Marble Church and details

If you are in the mood for admiring churches, then only a short distance from the Marble Church on the same side of Bredgade stands the Russian Orthodox **Alexander Newsky Kirke** (1883). However, the interior is closed to the public.

The doors to the Catholic **Skt Ansgar Cathedral** ❸❷ are open most afternoons (Tuesday to Sunday noon–4pm). This church suffered a similar fate to that of the Marble Church. None other than the Austrian Empress, Maria Theresia, acquired the land in 1774 and planned to build a grand church here. When she died in 1780, the money ran out and the chapel could not be furnished as grandly as intended. It was 1841 before private donations and the Catholic Church provided the necessary funds for the interior to be completed.

A few yards further along Bredgade, you will see a typical Frederiksstaden rococo building (1754). Now home to the ★ **Kunstindustrimuseet** ❸❸ (Tuesday to Friday 10am–4pm, Sunday 1–4pm), it was a hospital until 1910 and in 1919 it became the Museum of Decorative and Applied Arts. The principal attractions here are the collection of *objets d'art*, some fine French rococo furniture and various works by Danish designers. Its pretty garden is an inviting place to stop for a rest.

Kunstindustrimuseet: concert in the garden

Fredericiagade will take you away from Frederiksstaden. On the corner with Store Kongensgade, a shop sells Danish furniture and furnishings. On the same side of the street lies 'Ida Davidsen', one of the best *frokost* restaurants in town (*see page 80*).

The ★ **Nyboder** district with its humbler dwellings forms quite a contrast to sophisticated Amalienborg. Nyboder was built in the 1730s for seafarers and their families and some cottages in **Sankt Pauls Gade** (20–40) have retained their original design. They were built with one floor, but most of them have had extra floors added. In Nyboder itself, the more recent buildings are finished in an ochre/yellow shade, while in Rævegade to the north, the dark grey brick facades reflect the prevailing fashions of the late 19th century. The fascinating history of the Nyboder area is documented in the **Nyboder Mindestuer ❸❹** at Sankt Pauls Gade 20 (Wednesday noon–2pm, Sunday noon–4pm).

Sankt Pauls Kirke (1877) near the museum is sometimes used as a venue for concerts. It is almost as if time has stood still on the church square. Rather reminiscent of Carlsberg's Humleby (*see page 22*), there is a certain fragility about this quiet corner at the heart of a major European city. If you take a stroll around the area, you may come across Rosengade, one particularly idyllic retreat which certainly does justice to its 'green' name. During the next few years, it is intended that some of the street names be changed back to their original titles.

Kronprinsessegade leads back to Rosenborg Have. If you pass the entrance to the park, you will spot a dark, rather severe-looking building, which houses a unique museum. **Davids Samling ❸❺** (Tuesday to Sunday 1–4pm; admission free) keeps the art treasures that the lawyer, C.L. David, amassed. As well as European artworks and *objets d'art* from the 17th and 18th centuries, Scandinavia's finest collection of Middle Eastern art is displayed here.

Nyboder dwellings

Route 6

Along the transformed west bank

Nyhavn – Promenade – Gefionspringvand – Little Mermaid – Langeliniekaj – Frihavnen – Kastellet – Frihedsmuseet *See map on page 35*

Nowhere else in Copenhagen has changed as much as the port area. The traditional industries, such as ship-building, commerce and maritime travel, have collapsed and the B & W shipbuilding company on the east side of the port became insolvent in 1996, bringing to an end commercial activity in the city centre area. This tour shows what has become of the west side of the port. It largely follows the Langelinie coastal promenade – the old, defensive wall. While most of the warehouses and quayside installations have had to make way for change, the Little Mermaid looks on unimpressed.

Finish off the tour with a visit to the fascinating Freedom Museum, which documents the period of German occupation (1940–45). If you take a break in the pleasant quayside gardens, this will make a relaxing afternoon stroll – museum visits not included.

47

Set out for Kongens Nytorv, accessible by bus nos. 1, 6, 10, 27, 28 or 29 from City Hall Square.

At the spot where a huge anchor honours Danish sailors killed in World War II, Kongens Nytorv joins the short ★★ **Nyhavn** canal. The 'new' harbour was dug in 1671 to link Kongens Nytorv with the Øresund. In those days, rows of tall houses lined both sides of the waterway and in the warehouses and offices trade flourished. Sailors drank in the quayside taverns and, in its early days, Nyhavn was no place for respectable Copenhageners to take a quiet stroll. The maritime atmosphere was appreciated by artists though. Celebrated former residents include composer Daniel F.R. Kuhlau who lived at No. 23, man of letters Georg Brandes at No. 18 and fairytale writer Hans Christian Andersen who resided at No. 18, then No. 20 and, from 1848–67, at No. 67.

An anchor in honour of sailors

Nyhavn

Those tough times are now in the past, but the interest remains. Many of the facades on the sunny (northern) side are painted in bright, friendly colours and, during the warmer months, the canal banks are a veritable hive of activity.

It is not the place to find gourmet restaurants. What attracts locals and tourists alike is the hustle and bustle against a background of proud sailing ships. On sunny days, crowds swarm along the northern bank and pour in and out of the bars. Small boats ply up and down the

Nyhavn: a popular attraction

canal, which is a terminus for canalboat cruises as well as a hydrofoil service to Sweden.

Every visitor to Copenhagen will want to take home a snap of the bustling Nyhavn – and the best views are from the quieter south bank, where offices have largely replaced restaurants. Save the north side for an evening stroll, when it will probably be less frantic. You will soon pass in front of a side entrance to the baroque **Charlottenborg Slot**, since 1754 the home of the Royal Academy of Fine Arts (daily 10am–5pm). The palace was built at the end of the 17th century, shortly after Kongens Nytorv.

The **Nyhavnsbro** will take you over to the north side. On the way through to the Øresund, it is worth stopping to look at the house entrances and facades. Plaques, statues and stucco adornments remind visitors of celebrated former inhabitants including Hans Christian Andersen at No. 67. Some diving equipment, a relic from the 'Svitzer' rescue company which used to be based here, adorns the house on the corner of **Kvæsthusgade**.

At the end of the canal, look out for **71 Nyhavn Hotel**, an impressive example of how an old warehouse (1805) can be preserved. Above the wide windows, formerly openings for goods, the beam for supporting the lifting tackle is still visible.

The last remnant of the Baltic shipping trade is the **Kvæsthusbroen** landing stage, the departure point for ferries to Oslo and Bornholm. Vessels belonging to the Scandinavian Seaways company resemble a multi-storey office block laid on its side rather than a ship, but it is only with such huge capacity that ferry prices can stay at a reasonable level.

By the **Promenade** to the north of the Kvæsthusbroen peace returns. Many of the warehouses, some more than 200 years old, have been beautifully restored and have found new uses. The Copenhagen Admiral Hotel was once a grain store that itself developed out of two store-rooms in 1885.

Occupying the adjoining space and enclosed in concrete and marble, **Amaliehavn**, a rather sad green space with a fountain (1983) has never really been accepted by the local people. From here it is possible to view the Amalienborg palace square and the unmistakable copper dome of the Marble Church (*see page 45*). Probably the best facility in this garden is the kiosk where walkers can buy an ice-cream, before continuing their stroll along the promenade.

The scene would have been very different 200 hundred years ago – sailing ships would have been moored to the quayside, loading their cargo before setting sail to Green-

Amaliehavn

land or the Caribbean, and whalers would be returning from an arduous trip on the North sea. The three fine **Florentine-style warehouses**  date from around that time. Two of them were converted into apartments in the 1970s. The ground floor of the third warehouse contains the **Royal Casting Collection** (Wednesday and Thursday 10am–4pm, Saturday and Sunday 1–4pm) with casts of sculptures from various eras. A replica of Michelangelo's *David* stands in front of the building.

The Gefionspringvand

Florentine-style warehouses

On the other side of the Sound lies the extensive **Holmen** district, which the army cleared in 1995. Over the coming years, this area will undergo major changes.

Pass the Customs House and carry on towards the terminal for the ferry to the Polish port of Swinoujscie. Behind a wrought-iron gate, some way inland, tourists often gather to admire Copenhagen's most spectacular fountain, the ★ **Gefionspringvand** ❸. The sculptor, Anders Bundgaard, took 11 years to complete this colossal sculpture, which draws its inspiration from Nordic mythology. It symbolises the goddess, Gefion, who turned her four sons into bulls and attached them to a plough to drag the island of Sealand away from the Swedish mainland.

Not far from the splashing waters of the fountain stands **St Alban's Church** in English-inspired Gothic. Built between 1885 and 1887, it served to strengthen the ties between the Danish and British royal families. In 1863 Alexandra, the oldest daughter of Christian IX, married Edward, who later became King Edward VII. See the notice-board outside the church for opening times.

The Gefion Fountain marks the start of the Langelinie. Although this promenade is bordered by numerous sculptures, the prettiest, the most famous and now *the* symbol for Copenhagen is *Lille Havfrue* or the ★★ **Little**

Sport and relaxation on the quay

Mermaid 38 (*see picture on page 4*). Created by Edvard Eriksen and modelled on his wife, it depicts the tragic sea-maiden who exchanged her legs in order to win the love of an earthly prince, as recounted in one of Hans Christian Andersen's fairytales. Carl Jacobsen of Carlsberg Brewery fame commissioned the work and was responsible for specifying where it should be placed. It has graced the Langelinie since 1913. However, it is not the original sculpture. At one time the head was sawn off, and later the arm, but fortunately the original moulds have been kept and replacements have been made. The sculpture is smaller than most photographs make it appear.

The 1km (½-mile) long **Langeliniekaj** north of the yachting marina marks the end of the Langelinie. Built in 1894 at the same time as the neighbouring Frihavnen, it is the meeting point for modern cruise ships and antiquated freighters from all over the world.

For walkers, the best view of the comings and goings is from the raised, tree-lined promenade beside the asphalt track along the quay. This stretch of road is very popular with locals, who on summer weekends drive their cars onto the promenade, look out over the Øresund and enjoy *pølser* or ice-creams.

On the west side of the promenade, behind an ageing metal fence, lies the next destination. The **Frihavnen** (the Free Harbour) was completed in 1894. By the 1970s, the basin and facilities could no longer be used by modern freighters and container ships and so it was closed. Now it is a splendid example of how decaying industrial areas can be given a new lease of life. Around the edge of the eastern harbour, a fine new office and residential area made from glass, concrete and brick has been completed, although at the moment, the young trees are barely established and the whole site looks bare. One relic from the past remains: architect Dahlerup's ornate warehouse has been fully restored and will be resuming life as offices.

Return to the city centre via the **Kastellet** or Citadel, a key element in the establishment of the Langelinie. This installation goes back to the middle of the 17th century when, after the loss of the southern Swedish provinces, the city boundaries had to be moved outside the gates as a defence against unwanted visitors (*see page 10*). Frederik III ordered the construction of the defensive wall and citadel to guard the harbour entrance. In 1664, the first soldiers took up their positions in the Frederikshavn citadel, later known simply as Kastellet.

Ramparts and a moat surround the strictly symmetrical, star-shaped site. Leave the Frihavnen via the **Norgesport**. This grassy bank is now popular with mothers and pushchairs, dog-walkers and joggers, but the military are still there too. Renovated at the end of the 1980s, the barracks are out of bounds for the general public. Nevertheless, the soldiers and the public live together in harmony. In fact, it is the citadel church (1705), of all places, that enjoys popularity with couples about to marry. Sometimes on a Saturday afternoon, traffic jams form as wedding guests arrive and depart. Next to the church stands the detention centre (1725) where enemies of the state were held. Detainees have included traitors, disgraced dignitaries and, most recently, Werner Best, Hitler's commander in Denmark.

On a section of the ramparts above the church stands the third version of the citadel's own windmill (1847). This outpost was designed to be fully self-sufficient in the event of a siege, so the barracks did not just consist of accommodation and ammunition stores, but there were also tanks full of drinking water and even a bakery.

A cobbled road links the Norgesport with the **Sjællandsport** in the south. On the other side of the moat, a memorial commemorates those Danes who died during the period of German occupation (1940–45). It also marks the point where you can cross to the Churchillpark, the location for the ★★ **Frihedsmuseet ③** (1 May to 15 September Tuesday to Saturday 10am–4pm, Sunday 10am–5pm; otherwise Tuesday to Sunday 11am–4pm; admission free). This museum documents the activities of the Danish Resistance Movement during the German occupation (*see page 11*). Displays illustrate the daring exploits of the Danish activists, who spirited Jews across the border to Sweden, manned radio stations and operated printing presses. Others made weapons, committed acts of sabotage or fought alongside the Allies. Documents and newspaper cuttings show how the occupying forces reacted to the resistance movement.

Frihedsmuseet exhibits

51

Cruising the canal

Route 7

A break from the city

**Gammel Dok – Christianshavn Canal – Vor Frelsers
Kirke – Free State of Christiania – Christians Kirke
– B&W Museet** *See map on page 54*

The bridge by the old Stock Exchange leads across into
the Christianshavn district, where the pace of life visi-
bly slows. But you will soon see that modern building
styles have spread across the water, a fact demonstrated
by the singularly unattractive Foreign Ministry. Fortunately, a much more impressive architectural example occupies one of the best spots by the water's edge. Around

Lunch by the water

the quiet Christianshavn Canal, the landscape remains unchanged, although a whiff of decay pervades the air in
some places. This area is home to many ordinary folk as
well as some rather extraordinary ones. The Free State
of Christiania in the north-east celebrated its 25th anniversary in 1996 in the face of considerable hostility
and prophecies of doom. This tour of Christianshavn can
easily be completed on foot and will last about three hours.

Take bus no. 8 from the city centre. The **Knippelsbro**
bridges the Inderhavnen, the channel between the city centre and Christianshavn. Just to the left stand the bleak, grey
offices of the Danish Foreign Ministry (1980) – this huge
complex by Asiatisk Plads has little in common with the
rest of Christianshavn. The adjoining **Strandgade** provides clear evidence of how this quarter looked in its earlier days. Four hundred years ago, this area was nothing
but marshland with a few small islands. In order to create a harbour, between 1617 and 1622 thousands of tree

trunks were driven into the soil, much earth was shifted, a rectangular settlement created and named Christianshavn after the then king, Christian IV. A canal was dug in the Dutch style to divide the area into an upper and a lower town. Initially, Christianshavn was an independent municipality, but in 1682 it was annexed to Copenhagen, whereupon the settlement was extended and the unprotected east side was enclosed by a semi-circular wall. Although this quarter is considerably younger than the centre of Copenhagen, it boasts some of the city's oldest, terraced houses. A good example of the early buildings are Nos. 26–36 Strandgade, although admittedly new floors have been added and the frontages altered.

As the city's trading links developed at the beginning of the 18th century, new warehouses, offices, docks and workshops were built at the water's edge. **Asiatisk Plads** owes its name to the 'Asiatisk Kompagni', whose premises were grouped around a small harbour basin. On the north side of the square, the marble facade of the elongated rococo warehouse (designed by Nicolai Eigtved in 1750) dates from Christianshavn's heyday. Now fashionably restored, it is used as a conference centre.

Until 1918, a harbour lay on the other long side of the warehouse, but this was filled in. Today a car park occupies the site of Copenhagen's first dry dock (1739) for the repair and maintenance of sailing ships.

Little remains of the ★ **Gammel Dok** , the Old Dock, apart from its name. In the mid-1980s, the neighbouring warehouse (1882) was impressively restored. Unlike many similar projects, the public have access to the interior as it belongs to the **Danish Centre for Architecture** and is used as a venue for exhibitions (Dansk Arkitektur & Byggeeksport Center, daily 10am–5pm). With its bright rooms, exposed beams and newly laid wooden floors, there could be no better example of how to renovate an old building.

The Danish Centre for Architecture

From the quayside, the view encompasses Slotsholmen with the old Stock Exchange in the foreground. The 60-year-old Knippelsbro occupies the same site as all the other bridges that have linked the old town and Christianshavn.

Sadly, despite all the restored warehouses, the quayside is unable to recreate the old maritime atmosphere. No wooden sailing boats are moored alongside and no old seadogs sit by the water's edge with pipe in mouth. Only the excellent cafeteria in the Gammel Dok can offer any sustenance and that will be from a salad counter rather than a smoky, old sailors' bar.

Much more of a waterside feel surrounds the ★ **Christianshavn Canal**, where rows of pleasure boats bob up and down. The closer you get to the **Wildersbro** bridge, the

Christianshavn Canal

more evidence there is of better bygone days. On the right-hand side stands the orange-yellow **Pakhus 4**, another example of a successful conversion from warehouse to office block. Many of the facades in this quarter exhibit the same gaudy colour scheme. In the early 18th century, the opposite side of the canal was occupied by the premises of ship owner and timber-merchant Andreas Bjørn. The brick building in red and yellow housed the offices, the half-timbered structure next door was the sail-making workshop, while the company's own wharf suffered the same fate as the Gammel Dok and was filled in.

Take a right turn and follow the main canal which splits Christianshavn in half. The two narrow lanes on either side of the water, **Overgaden neden Vandet** (Lower Town) and **Overgaden oven Vandet** (Upper Town) are lined with more old warehouses, town houses and company headquarters. Rather than examining the various facades, it is perhaps more interesting to view the canal from the Skt Annæ Gade bridge. The boats tied up against the tree-lined banks make a picturesque sight, probably one of the most photogenic in Copenhagen. It is a relaxing spot where you could easily forget about the pulsating capital city only a few hundred yards away, were it not for the multi-lingual commentaries emanating from the tourist boats which pass underneath the bridge.

If you feel a few pangs of hunger and decide that you want more than just a quiet contemplative moment, take a few steps along Skt Annæ Gade as far as the corner of Wildersgade and call in for a mid-morning snack at the

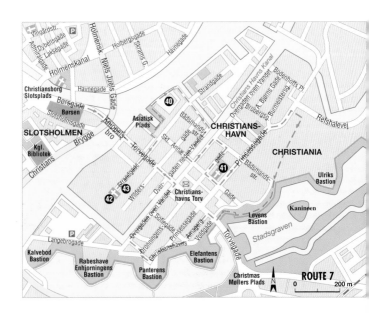

'Café Wilder' (*see page 81*), a popular haunt of the younger crowd.

Back in Overgaden oven Vandet, look out for No. 48. Peter Norden Sølling's portrait on the frontage was the work of Thorvald Bindebøll, son of the Slotsholmen architect, MG Bindebøll. The effects of the British bombardment (*see page 11*) disturbed Sølling, a generous man, and in 1819 he set up a fund to support the widows and families of seamen. He collected the money in the cylinder of a bomb which the British had fired, and this explains why the foundation went under the name of *Bombebøssen* (or 'bomb tin'). In 1891 No. 48 Overgaden oven Vandet became the new home of the foundation and the building has remained unaltered ever since, although the foundation is now based in the parallel Dronningensgade.

The elongated rococo building at Overgaden 58–64 has undergone many changes and has been put to numerous uses since it was built in 1754. After starting out as a school, it then served as a prison, a hospital and a rehabilitation centre for wounded naval personnel. It is now the **Orlogsmuseet** or Maritime Museum (Tuesday to Sunday noon–4pm), where ship models, uniforms, nautical instruments and weapons are housed. Probably the museum's most prized exhibit is the tiny submarine, which visitors can enter. With military music playing over the loudspeakers, it is in need of an update, so it is perhaps best saved for a rainy day.

Orlogsmuseet

55

Return to Skt Annæ Gade and on the left stands ★★ **Vor Frelsers Kirke** or Our Saviour's Church (1 March to 30 November, daily 9am–4.30pm; otherwise daily 10am–2pm; free admission to nave). The spire with its external staircase is a striking landmark and, if time permits, the climb to the top is well worth the effort, providing one of the finest views over Copenhagen.

Situated in this modest quarter, its opulent interior comes as something of a surprise. Among the most striking features are the monumental organ, supported by two large stucco elephants, the altar with its marble plinth and the reliefs on the pulpit balustrade. To make an ascent of the tower requires an exciting expedition through intricate roof timbers.

Vor Frelsers Kirke view

The unusual freedom statue on the corner of Prinsessegade and Bådsmandsstræde hints at a change of atmosphere. Just 100m (110yds) further up Prinsessegade appears the entrance to the ★ **Free State of Christiania**.

When in 1971 the Danish military abandoned the barracks on Bådsmandsstræde, property speculators started to rub their hands in anticipation, but their hopes of a quick profit were dashed when a group of alternative types, dropouts and hippies moved in and sought to realise their

The Free State of Christiana: an alternative lifestyle

Part of the cultural palette

No drugs

Sharing out the rations

idealistic notion of communal living. For 16 years, the properties were threatened with demolition, but in 1987 the Danish Parliament gave its approval to the self-appointed Free State, subject to the signing of an agreement about how the land could be used, as it still belongs to the Defence Ministry.

The agreements have now been signed, but conservative circles continue to display a hostile attitude to the residents. Critics complain primarily about the sale and use of marijuana and argue that the inhabitants represent a permanent threat to law and order. Be that as it may, Christiania now seems more secure than ever. This traffic-free area with its generous provision of nurseries and playgrounds is certainly ideal for children, who make up a large percentage of the inhabitants. Bicycles and restored ovens are exported to many parts of Europe and the 'Grønne Hal' market has been recycling building materials for several years. The 'Loppen' concert hall is a lively cultural centre and the 'Spiseloppen' restaurant is among the best in the city.

The democratically-elected assembly has made some difficult decisions: to counter the drug-pushers, the Christianiers have banned the sale and consumption of hard drugs and have evicted a gang of rockers who were seeking to gain control.

Visitors are invited to come and share a vegetarian meal, to take part in the community's cultural life or to stroll along the Stadsgraven moat. Cameras aren't particularly welcome, especially near where the drug pushers operate. Open Monday to Thursday noon–8pm, Friday noon–4pm. The best way to explore the Free State of Christiania is by joining an organised walking tour (Saturday and Sunday at 3pm). *Nitten* is an informative tourist guide with text in English.

You can continue along the ramparts straight from Christiania. **Christianshavns Vold** runs between Stadsgraven and **Christianshavns Voldgade** and provides a good view of the site. Only the Torvegade over to Amager interrupts the zigzag line of the ramparts with its five-cornered bastions, where the soldiers once stood guard.

The 100m (110yd) **Amagergade**, a turning off Torvegade which runs parallel to Voldgade, used to be the poorest street in the quarter. In the mid-19th century, almost 1,000 people were crammed into the insanitary dwellings and tuberculosis and other diseases were rife. Standing in front of these neat half-timbered houses, it is now hard to imagine the misery that the people had to endure. Further west the ramparts, canal and Overgaden oven Vandet converge. On the corner of Sofiegade is 'Sofies Kælder', an underground bar from which cheery mainstream jazz echoes every Sunday.

Return to Torvegade and on the right-hand side you will see **Christianshavn Torv** marketplace with a number of statues and an ancient, unused telephone kiosk. Torv and Torvegade serve as the district's main shopping streets.

Christianshavns Voldgade

57

The tour through Christianshavn begins and ends in Strandgade. At the far end stands ★ **Christians Kirke** ㊷ (1 March to 31 October, daily 8am–6pm; otherwise 8am–5pm; admission free). It was built between 1755 and 1759 at the same time as the grand buildings in Frederiksstaden, hence the familiar rococo style. Rather like a theatre, it has three galleries with boxes, which were set aside for the district's wealthy families.

Next to the church, where a brand new office block now occupies the best waterside location, were the dockyards of **Burmeister & Wain**, or B & W as the company was usually known. In 1996, precisely 150 years after it was established, B & W went into liquidation. Paddle steamers, ferries, luxury yachts, cruise liners, warships, container vessels and supertankers all slid off the slipway here. In fact, if it floated, B & W probably made it. However, despite a reputation for quality, the Danes could not compete against low-wage economies of the Far East or the subsidised shipyards of Germany. B & W was Copenhagen's last shipbuilder. Its vast yards on the island of Refshaleøen, north of Christianshavn, are now quiet. The loss of this vital industry was a disaster for the employees concerned, and also meant the city had to look hard at its own place in the world.

The **B & W Museet** ㊸, housed in an old warehouse, documents the history of the firm via models and photos of the finest, largest and most technically advanced vessels that left B & W's shipyards (Monday to Friday 10am–1pm; admission free).

The B&W Museet

Route 8

Frederiksberg

Københavns Bymuseum – Det Kongelige Danske Haveselskabets Have – Frederiksbergs Have – Zoologisk Have – Royal Copenhagen Porcelain Manufactory

Close to the City Museum runs the border between Copenhagen and Frederiksberg, a town within a town with a population of about 90,000. Unlike nearby Vesterbro, this area used to be favoured by the middle and upper classes, but it is now hard to tell the difference between Frederiksberg and Copenhagen. Visitors are particularly attracted to its extensive parks which surround the now fully restored Frederiksberg Palace and where Copenhagen Zoo is situated. Set aside a good half-day for this tour, longer if you intend to visit the zoo.

Take bus no. 27 or 28 from City Hall Square or Tivoli Gardens and alight near the City Museum. The more energetic may prefer to get around by bike.

Behind Tivoli Gardens and in front of the central station, you will pass the 15m (50ft) high sandstone **Frihedsstøtten** (1792–97), a column recalling the agricultural reforms of the 18th century which ended serfdom.

★ **Københavns Bymuseum ㊹** (1 May to 30 September, Tuesday to Sunday 10am–4pm, otherwise Tuesday to Sunday 1–4pm; admission free) occupies the former premises of the Royal Shooting Club (1786) at Vesterbrogade 59 in the north of Vesterbro. The City Museum's exhibits are particularly impressive for their originality and credibility, as, unusually, they focus not only on the glory days of the city's past, but also on the difficult periods in its development. It looks closely, for ex-

Københavns Bymuseum: delving into the past

ample, at the city around the middle of the 18th century, when, within the space of only a few decades, the population doubled. A small exhibition celebrates the intellectual contributions of Søren Kierkegaard, one of the city's most famous sons.

A clay model outside the museum shows what the city would have looked like around 1530 and the nearby cobbled Absalonsgade has been turned into a museum street where lanterns, fire hydrants and an Art Nouveau telephone kiosk covered with original advertising posters revive the atmosphere of the early 20th century.

Model of city around 1530

You will cross the boundary between Copenhagen and Frederiksberg just after the bus turns into **Frederiksberg Allé**, formerly Frederik IV's private road to his palace in Frederiksberg. It was 1862 before ordinary citizens were allowed to use this boulevard, which is lined by some fine patrician houses. Leave the bus before it has turned the corner, and before you stands the gateway into **Frederiksbergs Have**, the city's 'green lung'. However, before passing through the iron gates between the two lodges, it is worth making a short detour to the left. This small park, ★ **Det kongelige danske Haveselskabets Have ⓭** or the 'Garden of the Royal Danish Garden Society' is split into several sections, representing different types of landscaped gardens. It is a colourful, fastidiously tended jewel, where many delights await the visitor.

59

After Kongens Have near Rosenborg Castle (*see page 42*), the Copenhageners' favourite park is the spacious ★★ **Frederiksbergs Have** (daily from 6am until sunset. Chinese pavilion: 1 May to 30 September, Sunday 2–4pm).

Lazy days in Frederiksbergs Have

Inspired by many journeys to France and Italy, Frederik IV had the gardens laid out symmetrically in baroque style. **Frederiksberg Palace** (1703) overlooks the park from a hill in the south of the grounds. The gardens were redesigned in English style at the end of 18th century and Frederik's moats were dug out later and linked together into a system of canals, so in the summer visitors can enjoy a relaxing boat trip through the park. Crocuses, lilies, rhododendron, roses and lavender keep Frederiksbergs Have in colour throughout the summer months, but more flower-beds, huge trees, a fountain, artificial caves and little waterfalls add to its appeal. Families picnic and groups of children play on the grass, while sun-worshippers bask on regardless of all the chatter and laughter. On an island in the lake stands a pretty Chinese pavilion, where in the 19th century Frederik VI brought his family together for afternoon tea. In the eastern part of the park are three **Familiehaver ⓰** (family gardens), accessible only from Pille Allé, where you can enjoy typical Danish cuisine in the open air (mid-May to mid-September).

Frederiksberg Palace

Attention-seeking toucan

The zoo favourites

Royal Copenhagen porcelain

Frederiksberg Palace has undergone several facelifts since it was built and is now the home of the Danish army's Officers' Training School. It is not open to visitors.

Opposite the entrance to the palace lies the **Søndermarken,** a continuation of the Frederiksberg green belt. Between 1856 and 1859, what is now level grass was turned into several ponds, because the city was growing rapidly and the population faced serious water shortages. It was covered in 1889 for reasons of hygiene and this 4,500 sq.m (5,400 sq.yd) lake remained in use as a reservoir until 1981.

Copenhagen Zoo or ★ **Zoologisk Have** ❹❼ is located in the Frederiksbergs Have and Søndermarken area. At the entrance stands a mini-version of the Eiffel Tower which can be climbed for a few *krone*. Inside, the polar bears steal the show. The seal and penguin enclosures are also very popular at feeding time and there is a corner where young children can stroke the animals.

You can explore yet more of Frederiksbergs Have while en route to the next destination. There are some fine old linden trees on the **Mathildehøj** and a colony of herons on **Andebakkeøen Island**.

When you reach Smallegade, turn left for the entrance to the ★ **Royal Copenhagen Porcelain Manufactory** ❹❽ (factory tours: Monday to Friday at 9am, 10am, 11am, 1pm and 2pm. Shop in Fasanvej round the corner open Monday to Friday 9am– 5.30pm, Saturday 9am–2pm, *see also page 85*)

During a tour of the works which takes about an hour, visitors can become familiar with the product range and can also watch the artists at work. Almost a third of the workers here are artists. To be able to paint one of the costlier items, the craftsmen must undergo a full seven years of training. Some pieces require over 1,000 brushstrokes. Although the products are mainly china for everyday use, prices are sky-high, but visitors touring the factory have the opportunity to visit the shop which sells seconds discounted at between 30 and 40 percent. As well as china, the shop also sells crystal glass in modern designs.

Royal Copenhagen 'Blue Fluted' dinner services have been in production virtually unchanged since 1775. The painting method is the same as that used on Meissen pottery and that in turn originated in China. Experience proved that cobalt blue retained its colour well during the firing process. 'Flora Danica' (1789) is another well-known pattern. This new design was ordered by King Christian VII as a present for the Russian tsarina, Katharina II, but she died before the 1,800-piece set was finished. The motifs of the natural world were taken from *Flora Danica*, the Danish botanical encyclopaedia.

Route 9

Kalvebod Fælled nature reserve

Amager – the city's offshore island

Kalvebod Fælled – Kongelunden – Søvang – Dragør – Store Magleby – Amager Beach *See map on page 62*

61

For centuries, the 65 sq.km (25 sq.mile) island of Amager has supplied farm produce to the Danish capital. Paradoxically, Copenhagen has said thank you by creating a series of environmental problems on what was formerly a quiet retreat for its inhabitants. First of all there is Kastrup airport with its noisy planes landing and taking off, then there is all the airport road traffic, plus heavy goods vehicles coming off the E20 motorway and heading for the car ferry across the Øresund to Malmö and then, more recently, all the construction work connected with the new tunnel/bridge to Sweden, which is expected to open in 2000. Nevertheless, the southern part of the island is blessed with fascinating nature reserves and also some pretty villages, which have retained their rural character. To make the most of this tour, take a car or a bike, but bus numbers 30 and 33 also cover most of the route. If you like exploring, then allow a full day. Set out from the 'Bella Center' trade fair centre.

Taking it easy

One kilometre (about ½-mile) beyond the Bella Center, the Kongelundsvej branches off the main road and crosses the motorway. This new route cuts across the flat and uncultivated **Kalvebod Fælled** in the west of the island. For a period after World War II, Kalvebod Fælled, largely marshland drained by ditches, was used throughout the year as a training ground for Danish troops. It then became a bird and nature reserve and its network of paths is ideal for cyclists and energetic walkers, but take a good map as it is inadequately signposted. In addition, parts of the reserve are out of bounds as the army left behind countless unexploded shells.

The new motorway has reduced the area of this unspoilt reserve quite considerably but environmentalists hope that the bird-life will not be affected. Kestrels, buzzards, short-eared owls, hen-harriers and many other bird species either overwinter here or stay for the whole year. The car park by Frieslandsvej is a good starting place from which to explore the region. Alternatively, you can combine a tour of the Kalvebod Fælled with the neighbouring Kongelunden woodlands.

Until 200 years ago Amager had few trees, so firewood and timber for construction work were always in short supply. Several areas near **Kongelunden** were therefore turned into forest. The land passed to the king in 1836 and he set up wild pheasant farms so that wealthy Copenhageners could enjoy a day's shooting. In 1920, the King's

One species among many

ROUTE 9

0   2 km

Køge Bugt

Forest was opened up to the public and walkers are still likely to encounter pheasants scratching around in the undergrowth.

The memorial near the car park and bus stop remembers one of the royal hunters. Straight forest tracks run westward towards the Amager coastline and the treeless coastal strips, where in autumn birds gather before heading south. It is possible to gain access to the larger Kalvebod Fælled reserve via an embankment to the north-west of the woodland.

If you want to tour Amager by bike, you will have to be fairly fit, but if the opportunity arises, cycle along the coastal path to Dragør from **Søvang** and enjoy the splendid views. In Søvang, smart, highly desirable seaside cottages with neat gardens overlook the Øresund and in the summer the beach here is very popular with bathers.

Dragør detail

The picturesque town of ★★**Dragør** is the main attraction on Amager. Once a busy fishing and commercial port, it is now associated in most Danes' minds with the ferries to Malmö in southern Sweden. Every day, crowds of thirsty Swedes come over the Sound to load up with boxes of beer, markedly cheaper than in their own shops. To round off their trip, the Swedes usually end up on the terrace of the 'Dragør Strandhotel', enjoying to the full the cheaper Danish beer.

63

Amagermuseet: costume display

Diagonally opposite stands the oldest house in Dragør (1682), which is now a **local history museum** (1 May to 30 September, Tuesday to Friday 2–5pm, Saturday and Sunday noon–6pm). On more than one occasion, fires have badly damaged the Old Town – the last was in 1988 – but every time the architects manage to bring it back to life, ensuring that the reconstruction merges with the pretty, yellow-painted cottages.

The **Amagermuseet** ○ in **Store Magleby** in Hovedgaden (1 May to 30 September, Tuesday to Sunday noon–4pm; otherwise Wednesday and Sunday noon–4pm) reflects the Dutch influence on the island. In the 1520s Christian II brought Dutch farmers – noted for their farming expertise – to Amager to ensure that Copenhagen was always well supplied with farm produce. The two thatched farmsteads provide an appropriate setting for the agricultural collection.

Amager Strand lies to the north of Kastrup airport. **Øresund Udstilling** ○ in Kastrup yachting marina (1 May to 30 September, daily 10am–8pm; otherwise Tuesday to Sunday 10am–5pm) provides background information on the new tunnel and bridge project which in the year 2000 will link the European mainland to the Scandinavian sub-continent.

A day at the beach

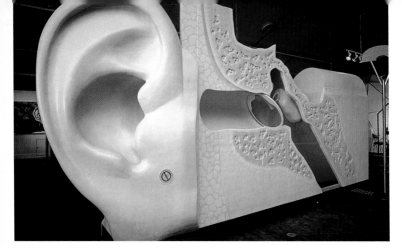

Among the organs at the Eksperimentarium...

Excursion 1

Taking it easy in the North

Eksperimentarium – Danmarks Akvarium – Charlottenlund Slotspark – Charlottenlund Strandpark – Bakken – Jægersborg Dyrehave *See map on page 67*

The northern districts of Gentofte, Charlottenlund and Klampenborg are where most wealthy Copenhageners live. Strandvejen, the coast road that runs beside the Øresund as far as Helsingør, is lined by grand villas, usually set back behind a wide green strip.

But this area is by no means an exclusive enclave for the better-off. As well as an attractive golf course, yachting marinas and a racetrack, numerous other places offer rest and recreation to everyone, whatever the size of their pocket.

The ★ **Experimentarium** (Monday, Wednesday to Friday 9am–5pm, Tuesday 9am– 9pm, Saturday and Sunday 11am–5pm; bus no. 6 from City Hall Square) is situated in the northern district of Hellerup in a wing of Copenhagen's last Tuborg brewery. It sets out to explain a variety of scientific principles, frequently using hands-on techniques. The enormous 4,000 sq metre hall contains some 300 or so demonstrations, all of which are sponsored by private industry.

'Learn by doing' is the message for everyone and you can test the capacity of your lungs, devise a calorie plan to suit your own body, carry out a drinking-water test, establish the radioactivity of naturally-occurring substances or look at various ways of saving energy. Cell research, communication and data transfer, air and water,

Where you can learn by doing

energy and environmental protection, nutrition and the workings of various human organs are just some of the topics which the inquisitive visitor can explore.

Special educational programmes have been devised and so school parties make up most of the visitors on weekdays. Temporary exhibitions – with experimentation as the main theme – are also held during the year.

In a country like Denmark, which is surrounded by the sea, aquaria are quite common, but ★ **Danmarks Akvarium** (1 March to 15 October, daily 10am–6pm; otherwise Monday to Friday 10am–4pm, Saturday and Sunday 10am–5pm; S-train to Charlottensund station, then an 800m (875yd) walk via Jægersborg Allé or bus no. 6 from City Hall Square) is still unique. Beautifully designed pools contain marine fauna from all over the world. Large landscaped tanks, which require the filtration of 300,000 litres (66,000 gallons) of water, recreate those distant continents, where piranha fish bare their frightening teeth or motionless crocodiles await the arrival of their next meal.

Danmarks Akvarium

As well as attempting to provide the fish and reptiles with their natural habitat, the aquarium also seeks to enlighten visitors by explaining some of the residents' little quirks. What, for example, are the secrets of the snapping turtle, why and how does the electric eel transmit electric impulses or why does the huge sea bass seem so unperturbed by the narrow confines of its tank? Another interesting display explains the food chain from plankton right through to predatory fish.

Denmark's aquarium is situated in **Charlottenlund Slotspark** by Strandvejen. This baroque castle was commissioned by Frederik IV for his daughter Charlotte Amalie in 1730, but the striking dome was not added until 1881.

Charlottenlund Slotspark

Charlottenlund Fort on the other side of Strandvejen was built between 1886 and 1888 as part of a fortification system to protect the entrance to Copenhagen's harbour. Abandoned in 1932, the site was integrated into the new **Charlottenlund Strandpark**, now one of the most popular beaches on Sealand. Part of it also serves as a campsite in the summer.

Charlottenlund Strandpark

The elegant suburb of Klampenborg is bordered to the north by a large, wooded area and the ★ **Bakken** pleasure park (end of March to end of August, daily 2pm–midnight; S-train to Klampenborg station and then 800m/875yds on foot via the Dyrehavsvej or bus no. 6 from City Hall Square). This site with its proud, 400-year-old tradition lies close to **Kirsten Pils Kilde**, a spring whose water was said to have medicinal powers. A market offering food, drink and entertainment was established near the

Souvenir hats

spring. It later moved to a hill and this hill gave its name to the fair. Bakken is perhaps more of a genuine funfair than Tivoli; it is certainly less sophisticated. Pierrot, the clown, awaits the children in his little cabin, and performers and musicians play on the open-air stage. The other 100 or so attractions include a roller-coaster, dodgems, swing-boats, white-water rides, shooting-ranges, modern rides and amusement arcades.

Few tourists find their way to Bakken. But as a straightforward funfair, it draws Copenhageners from all walks of life. However, unlike many such fairs, the food on offer here is generally well regarded. Admission to Bakken is free and the average cost of rides and food is well below that at Tivoli.

Bakken Hill forms the southern edge of what used to be the royal hunting grounds, ★ **Jægersborg Dyrehave**. Frederik III was happy with a small reserve, but his son, Christian V, was a keen hunter, and after his coronation in 1670, he enlarged the grounds so that prey could be rounded up and driven towards the hunters. Forestry workers and hunters throughout Denmark were obliged to catch red deer and bring them to Jægersborg Dyrehave. The monarch's passion for hunting was to be his downfall – he died in a hunting accident in 1699.

Deer in Jægersborg Dyrehave

In 1756 Frederik V opened up the spacious woodland to the public. Many of the trees, mainly beeches, oaks and other deciduous species, are over 200 years old and stand a good 50m (165ft) high. Dyrehave, now the biggest recreational area within greater Copenhagen, is criss-crossed by a network of footpaths, bridle paths and wide tracks. During the summer you can take a ride through the forest in a horse-drawn carriage. Starting out from Bakken funfair, the fare is very reasonable.

If you feel like exploring the area on foot, keep left at the horse-drawn carriages, carry on for a few yards and you will pass the Kirsten Pils Kilde spring. Then at the second junction, turn right. A little further on, the **Ulvedalene** valley opens out on the left. This area was used as an open-air theatre from 1910 to 1949, but in 1996, the tradition was revived for the Cultural Capital of Europe festivities and the national drama *Elverhøj* was performed in the Ulvedalene.

The Eremitagen

Turn right, left and then right again at the subsequent crossroads and follow a wide track as far as the **Eremitagen** hunting lodge (1736). The splendid view from this hilltop extends over the Øresund and there is also a good chance that you will see red deer grazing on the broad meadows. Two paths downhill, parallel to the track, will bring you back to Bakken.

Excursion 2

Out and about on North Sealand

Karen Blixen Museet – Louisiana – Frederiksborg Slot
– Roskilde Cathedral – Viking Ship Museum – Museet
for Moderne Kunst

If you have only a week to spend in Copenhagen, then you
will have to be selective. But if you're in the city for two
weeks, then you'll certainly have time for one or two day
trips into the Sealand hinterland.

Karen Blixen Museet

Karen Blixen was the sort of person who courted controversy. In her work she was not concerned with social
or psychological realism. For her, the questions that mat-
tered were 'Why is man on earth?' or 'What does God

Karen Blixen in conversation

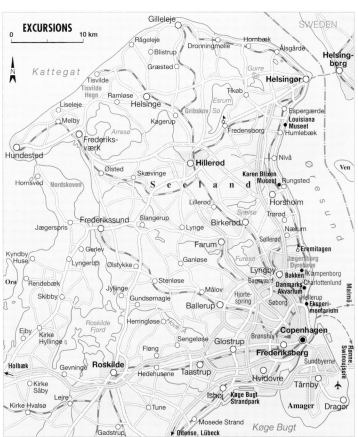

want from man?' Although Blixen's stylised language is not easy to penetrate, the success of her books demonstrates that she did strike a chord with her readers. But many Danes disdained the baroness's superior attitude. Blixen insisted on being addressed by her title, she always dressed elegantly and spoke in a strictly correct, rather old-fashioned style. It is often forgotten, however, that she was one of the first Danes to take issue on women's rights.

From 1914 to 1931 Blixen lived as a coffee grower in East Africa, where she wrote her most successful novels. When she returned to Denmark, she settled at her parents' home in **Rungstedlund**, north of Copenhagen. In 1991 the house was converted into a fascinating ★ **museum** (1 May to 30 September, daily 10am–5pm; otherwise Wednesday to Friday 1–4pm, Saturday and Sunday 11am–4pm) which sheds further light on the intriguing personality of Denmark's most celebrated female literary figure. To get to Rungstedlund take the S-train to Lyngby, then bus no. 388.

Louisiana

In the mid-1950s, the cheesemaker Knud W. Jensen walked the length of the Øresund coast in search of a suitable spot to realise his life-long dream. By his mid-40s, after successfully running a cheese factory, he was looking towards the art world for a new career. After buying a summer villa and parkland near Humlebæk, he began work on his project. Since 1958, ★★★ **Louisiana Museum of Modern Art** (Thursday to Tuesday 10am–5pm, Wednesday 10am–10pm) has become a superb platform for modern art from all over the world and it continues to go from strength to strength.

To get to Louisiana, take the train to Humlebæk and then bus no. 388.

Louisiana sculptures...

Although this open-air art gallery receives donations from other sources, Jensen allocated much of his fortune to the Louisiana foundation and the state pays for some of the running costs. Louisiana is no enclave for head-in-the-clouds artists. Its aim is to bring art to the whole of the community, irrespective of age and background. Louisiana is not just a home for modern art, it is a work of art in itself, aiming to show the 'interplay between art, architecture and the landscape'. Several unusual museum buildings are spread out across the site near Humlebæk some 40km (25 miles) north of Copenhagen, right next to the Øresund coast.

...and more sculptures

The park consists of a harmonious array of mature shrubs, lines of reeds, neatly tended lawns and stately beeches, planes and pines with modern sculptures dotted amongst them, often occupying surprising, but always visually pleasing locations. Art and landscape merge to create a natural atmosphere. With visitors relaxing on the grass or bathing in the lakes, it is easy to forget that this is a museum. Enjoy a picnic by a Moore, a Miró or an Arp and look across the Sound to Sweden. This is art in unison with nature.

69

The majority of the museum's treasures – mostly paintings, prints and sculptures – are kept in the two main buildings and in the pavilions, linked by airy promenades which help to bring nature closer. As the route changes, visitors find themselves below ground one minute and then suddenly startled by skilfully designed lighting. Who knows what waits round the corner? It seems to lack order and yet the surroundings subtly evoke the spirit of Picasso, Max Ernst, Asger Jorn and other CoBrA artists, Warhol, Rauschenberg, Calder, Giacometti and many others. Special exhibitions are also held here.

Frederiksborg Slot

After Rosenborg Castle, ★★ **Frederiksborg Castle** (1 May to 30 September, daily 10am–5pm; April and October daily 10am–4pm; otherwise daily 11am–3pm) is probably the finest royal palace on Sealand. Situated 35km (22 miles) northwest of Copenhagen near **Hillerød**, it can be reached by S-train to Hillerød station, then bus no. 701, 702 or 703.

Frederiksborg Slot: interior

At the start of the 17th century, Christian IV transformed his father's castle into a grand Renaissance-style castle, standing astride three tiny islands in Hillerød's town lake. The Dutch Renaissance with its red bricks, bright sandstone and arching gables is immortalised here. Some sections of the sandstone adornments were gilded and painted. Frederik VII was the last monarch to reside at Frederiksborg. When a fire damaged the main block in 1859, he ordered it to be rebuilt, but restricted finances slowed down progress and, when Frederik died in 1863, work stopped completely. A begging bowl had to be rattled in front of some distinguished benefactors before the castle was saved from further decline. It finally re-opened in 1884 as the Danish National History Museum, to be administered by the Carlsberg foundation. Now visitors can explore more than 70 magnificent rooms, including the Audience Room, the Knights' Hall, the Royal Wing, the Princes' Wing and the old church. As well as paintings and royal portraits, many valuable pieces of furniture have found a fitting home here.

Roskilde Cathedral: details

Roskilde

According to legend, the Viking king Roar founded the town of Roskilde (pop. 50,000) just under 30km (19 miles) to the west of Copenhagen at the southern end of **Roskilde-fjord** around 600, making it one of Denmark's oldest towns. It was none other than the founder of Copenhagen, Bishop Absalon, who commissioned ★★★ **Roskilde Cathedral** around 1170. In the 13th century, the original Romanesque building was drastically altered to give the red-brick cathedral a French Gothic appearance. The cathedral's distinctive spires were added in 1635. Over the centuries, the cathedral was extended to accommodate several burial chapels, the resting places for a total of 38 kings and queens, some of whose sarcophagi are extravagantly decorated.

A tour around the interior provides a lesson in Danish history. The first king to be buried here was Harald I (d. 985) and the last was Frederik IX (d. 1972). When furnishing the interior, only the best was good enough. Of particular note are the carved choir stalls (1420), the clock with the moving figures (c. 1500), the gilded high altar (late 16th century) and the remarkable bookstands in the chancel. During the summer, the baroque Raphaelis organ (1554) is used for organ recitals. The Absalon arch, a relic from the first chapel (c. 1200) links the cathedral with the palace, formerly the bishops' residence (open 1 April to 30 September, Monday to Friday 9am–4.45pm, Saturday 9am–noon, Sunday 12.30–4.45pm; otherwise Tuesday to Friday 10am–3.45pm and Saturday and Sunday as long as no church services are taking place; train to Roskilde or bus no. 123, 210 or 600).

In 1962 some extraordinary excavation work started in the Roskildefjord after archaeologists discovered the remains of several Viking ships. The ships were probably scuttled in the fjord between 1000 and 1050. It took a great deal of meticulous work first to remove the fragments from the mud and stones and then to conserve them. The results of all the laborious treatment can be seen in the ★★ **Viking Ship Museum** (Vikingeskibshallen, 1

Part of the Viking heritage

70

April to 31 October, daily 9am–5pm; otherwise 10am–4pm; train to Roskilde, then bus no. 358).

There are five ships altogether, all of different kinds, and they include an ocean-going merchant ship, a warship and an inshore boat which probably served as a ferry as well as a fishing boat.

From the glass facade of the Viking Ship Museum it is possible to look out over the fjord, where reconstructions of Viking ships float on the water. During the summer they are used to take visitors for a trip on the fjord. Models, videos, special exhibitions and a fascinating film showing how the boats were salvaged also form part of the museum.

Museet for Moderne Kunst

In order to boost the culturally barren southern environs of Copenhagen, the ★★ **Museum of Modern Art** (Tuesday to Sunday 10am–5pm, Wednesday until 9pm) was opened in 1996 in **Ishøj Strandpark** by the Baltic coast. Take the S-train to Ishøj station, then bus no. 218.

Nicknamed the 'Ark', this bold concrete design, appropriately in the shape of a ship's hull, merges well with the surrounding countryside. The main art axis, which extends for the full length of the 'Ark' (140m/460ft), serves as the hub for all the other rooms. Concrete walls, some 12m (40ft) high, and huge, riveted steel plates lend a harsh, uncompromising feel to the art axis, while the side rooms at various levels – enhanced by subtle use of light – create a playful effect.

The bold and unusual design of the interior provides an ideal setting for the avant-garde works of art displayed here. As the museum's own collection is currently rather modest, temporary exhibitions are often the main focal point of a visit.

Museet for Moderne Kunst

Art, Literature and Music

*Opposite: detail of a
Thorvaldsen sculpture*

Only after the Napoleonic War, when the people started to acquire a genuine sense of national identity, did Danish art begin to develop its own stylistic qualities. Previously, most artists, mainly painters and writers, had been swept along by central European currents and patrons of the arts usually commissioned foreign artists and architects. The heyday of Danish art and culture is now referred to as the 'Golden Age' *(Guldalder)*.

Painting and sculpture

Copenhagen Art Academy, an institution founded in 1754, where most Danish painters and sculptors received their basic education, laid the foundations for the 'Golden Age'. The self-confidence of the artists who studied here was boosted by the fact that their academic mentor, the sculptor Bertel Thorvaldsen (1770–1844), had won international acclaim in Rome and was sought after by prestigious collectors from all over the world. Thorvaldsen now has his own museum in Copenhagen (*see Route 3, page 31*).

*Alexander Calder sculpture
at Louisiana*

73

The painter, Christoffer Wilhelm Eckersberg (1783–1853) earned his first plaudits abroad. When he returned home in 1816 and became a professor at the Art Academy, the Royal Court commissioned him to paint historic paintings for the Christiansborg Palace. During his leisure time, he painted in the open air. These naturalistic works and Eckersberg's precise technique explain his special place in the Danish art world. In addition, he influenced a whole generation of young artists, who formed the 'hard core of the Golden Age' and included Christen Købke (1810–48), who concentrated on Danish themes and often painted in Copenhagen. It is interesting to compare the castle today with his paintings.

At the end of the 19th century the Skagen school of painters – named after the artists' colony in northern Jutland – turned their backs on the teachings of the Art Academy and became Denmark's principal exponents of Impressionism. Peter Severin Krøyer (1851–1909) and Anna Ancher (1859–1935) were the leading figures in the movement. Den Hirschsprungske Samling Museum (*see Route 4, page 39*) contains a good cross-section of their work.

CoBrA (Copenhagen-Brussels-Amsterdam), an international group formed by the painter Asger Jorn (1914–73), disregarded academic tradition and devoted itself to abstract art. Jorn did not bother with preparatory sketches and painted spontaneously. But improvisation and experimentation were poorly received in respectable Danish art circles and in 1953 Jorn left the country.

During the 1960s, the private Experimental Art School came under the spotlight. Its most prominent member, the Copenhagen painter and sculptor Per Kirkeby (born 1938), started out as a experimental artist, joined the international art circle Fluxus and, during the 1970s, worked as a film producer. He has published a series of poetry books and is currently working as an architect. In 1987 he won the Thorvaldsen medal, the highest fine art award in the country.

The most comprehensive collection of 19th- and 20th-century Danish art is to be found in Copenhagen's Statens Museum for Kunst (*see Route 4, page 39*), the above-mentioned Hirschsprungske Samling and the privately-run Ny Carlsberg Glyptotek (*see Route 3, page 25*). The unusual Louisiana Museum of Modern Art, to the north of Copenhagen (*see Excursion 2, pages 68–9*), has the finest collection of contemporary international art, while the younger generation of Danish artists display their works in the new Museet for Moderne Kunst in Ishøj (*see Excursion 2, page 71*).

Statens Museum for Kunst

Literature

Denmark's first, internationally-recognised literary figure was Ludvig Holberg (1684–1754), a dramatist, lyricist and a professor at Copenhagen University. He produced a wealth of comedies, albeit with a serious message, and his work was performed at Denmark's first national theatre. He enjoyed great success with his Utopian story *Nicolai Klim's Underground Journey* (1741), in which he appointed himself as a spokesman for religious tolerance. Holberg wrote the novel in Latin, so that he could maximise his readership, but it was immediately translated into German, Dutch, French, English, Danish and Swedish, and later into Russian and Hungarian. It is still widely available.

Hans Christian Andersen and a fairytale set at the Tivoli

Hans Christian Andersen (1805–75) gave folk tales a new, humorous twist. Between 1835 and 1875, he published no fewer than 150 fairytales with *Tin Soldier*, *The Ugly Duckling*, and *The Emperor's New Clothes* among the best known. Andersen came from a poor background and had to wait some time for recognition. He initially hoped for a career on the stage and only later did he discover his talent for writing. He lived in Copenhagen from 1819 onwards.

The philosopher Søren Kierkegaard (1813–55) lived most of his life in Copenhagen. His literary works were unique and he cannot be categorised under the usual aesthetic criteria as his writings consist of essays, philosophical analyses, polemics, literary criticism, psychological dissertations and religious theses. What is notable about Kierkegaard is not just his remarkable command of language, but also the complex structure of his works – something which unfortunately renders them inaccessible to some readers.

Georg Brandes (1842–1927) represents the transition from Romanticism to Naturalism. This literary critic, essayist and (from 1902) professor at Copenhagen University expected the literature of the time to address contemporary problems in society and wanted to bid farewell to Romantic idealism. Brandes influenced such writers as Jens Peter Jacobsen (1847–85), Hermann Bang (1857–85) and also the Norwegian Henrik Ibsen (1826–1906).

Martin Andersen Nexø (1869–1954) devoted himself to social criticism. His book *Pelle the Conqueror* (1906–10; 4 parts) describes poverty and exploitation among Danish peasants in the late 19th century. With its first-hand description poverty as well as the growth of the labour movement, it was regarded by the socialist movement as a heroic epic. For a long time, however, Nexø was denied recognition by Danish literary circles.

Initially, Karen (Tania) Blixen (1885–1962) also had a difficult time in her native country. The greatest female writer in Danish literary history, she was a colourful personality with immense talent as a storyteller. Her 1938 novel *Out of Africa* provided the inspiration for a spectacular film in 1985 in which Meryl Streep romanced with Robert Redford. Blixen's farmstead in Rungstedlund is now a museum (*see Excursion 2, pages 67–8*).

Contemporary Danish literature has fought bravely on the international book market and has probably won proportionately more than its fair share. Pia Tafdrup, Inger Christensen, Henrik Stangerup and Klaus Rifbjerg are the established leaders, with Peter Høeg a name that has emerged in the 1990s. His subtle *Miss Smilla's Feeling for Snow* has had quite an impact on Danish literature and in 1997 *Smilla's Sense of Snow* became a Hollywood movie starring Vanessa Redgrave.

Concertgoers on Rådhuspladsen

Music

Secular music was encouraged in the Royal Court during the 16th and 17th centuries. It maintained a choir of trained singers, an instrumental ensemble and a trumpet band. Christian IV (1588–1648) was the first king to bring renowned, foreign composers to Copenhagen. Extravagant dramatic works with music were staged, with French-style ballet, orchestral music and, from 1689, opera, among the most popular productions.

Classical Viennese music, including the work of Haydn and Mozart, dominated the first third of the 19th century. Beethoven's compositions were only occasionally heard, usually on the initiative of Daniel Friedrich

Rudolph Kuhlau (1786–1832). Kuhlau wrote operas, and also the score for Johan Ludvig Heiberg's *Elverhøj* and he occupies a prominent place in the history of Danish music.

Carl August Nielsen (1865–1931) is another leading name. He not only wrote operas, symphonies, violin concertos and compositions for piano, but as the conductor of the Copenhagen Court Ensemble from 1907 to 1914 and then as director of the Copenhagen Conservatory, he also exerted a tremendous influence on the development of music in Denmark.

Per Nørgard (born 1932) is the principal exponent of Danish avant-garde music, but Ib Nørholm, Gunnar Berg, Pelle Gudmundsen-Holmgreen, Flemming Weis and Niels Viggo Bengtsson also deserve a mention. Since the 1960s, Copenhagen has had a reputation for jazz, due in part to the brilliant American jazz saxophonist Ben Webster, who lived in the city. Jazz clubs and an annual Jazz Week continue the tradition. The calendar for rock and pop is equally lively, with concert venues and many pubs also providing a stage for established and up-and-coming groups (*see Leisure, page 83*).

Ben Webster

76

Cinema

At the end of the 19th century, the new medium of moving pictures aroused considerable interest in Denmark. Copenhagen's first cinema, the 'Kosmorama' opened in 1904. Ole Olsen (1863–1943), one of the first cinema owners, invested a lot of money in the industry and in 1906 he founded the 'Nordisk Films Kompagni', which is still in existence today and said to be the oldest film company in the world. He had a studio built and employed the best producers and actors. Olsen extended his empire into Germany and Russia and up until World War I 'Nordisk' occupied a powerful position. By World War II, however, it had lost its markets outside Scandinavia as the best actors and actresses went abroad.

It was the late 1980s before Danish film-makers reappeared on the international stage with works such as *Babette's Feast* and Bille August's *Pelle the Conqueror*; both won Oscars for the Best Foreign Film. Bille August has since made such films as *The Best Intentions*, based on Ingmar Bergman's script, *The House of the Spirits*, and *Smilla's Feeling for of Snow* and now ranks among the world's leading film producers.

A new generation of Danish producers have been winning plaudits. In 1996, for example, Lars von Trier won a prize at the Cannes Film Festival with *Breaking Waves*. Breaking with tradition yet again, both Lars von Trier and Lars Winterberg have taken to using hand-held cameras and no additional lighting.

Events Calendar

Below is a list of some of the main events that take place in Copenhagen. Most of the annual festivals involve music. Many museums hold special art and sculpture exhibitions, but these will be at irregular intervals and usually on specific themes. For further details, contact the Tourist Office (*see pages 90–91*).

January: Venue Rock Festival, underground rock on the last weekend of January. At the usual rock venues.

End of April/beginning of May: 'Golden Days in Copenhagen' recalls the Golden Age with theatre, ballet and concerts, walking tours of the city and excursions. Full programme of events in the Tourist Office or at 'Golden Days in Copenhagen', Stockholmsgade 20, 2100 Copenhagen Ø, fax: 31 42 14 91.

Whitsuntide: 'Karneval i København', carnival processions and concerts (rock, blues, folk and jazz). In the Fælledpark, Rosenborg Have and the inner city.

End of June: Roskilde Festival, the country's biggest rock festival for over 100,000 music fans. A long weekend in a country park Woodstock-style.

Beginning of July: Copenhagen Jazz Festival with bands playing every jazz style from bebop onwards. On stage, in pubs and on the streets.

Mid-August–beginning of September: 'Glyptotekets Sommerkoncerter', classical music in the Ny Carlsberg Glyptotek.

Festival city

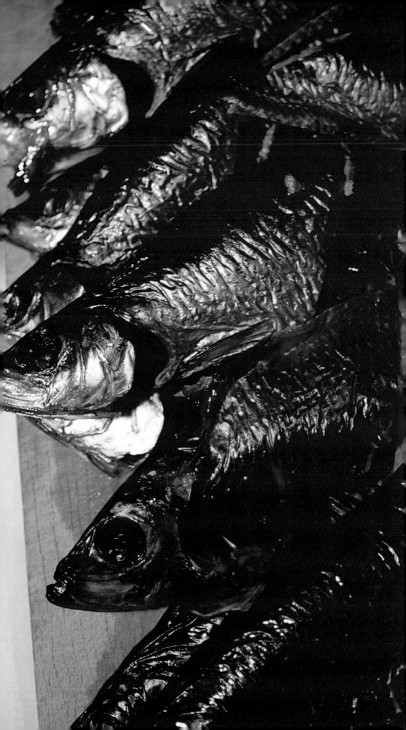

Food and Drink

The Danes like to think of themselves as the 'French of the north'. Food and drink are important for their quality of life. They believe in 'living to eat' not 'eating to live'.

Visitors will soon come to appreciate that unique Danish creation, *smørrebrød* or 'bread and butter', but do not be misled by this oversimplification. The bread, thickly-spread with butter, forms the basis for open sandwiches topped with salmon, eel, plaice, herring, beef, liver pâté, ham, steak tartare, egg, cheese, chicken breast, turkey or seafood and then garnished with sauces and vegetables, salads and herbs. The usual time for a *smørrebrød* is midday as a *frokost* or 'second breakfast'. Copenhagen boasts several specialist *frokost* restaurants which usually open from 10am to 5pm to serve mainly city workers. Many *frokost* restaurants prepare the toppings and the guest selects the type of bread, topping, sauce or marinade at the bar by marking a list; a pair of skilful hands will then make up the snack. There are also self-service counters, where you can buy a ready-made *smørrebrød* to take away.

Smørrebrød ingredients

The proper name for lunch is *middag*, although it is usually a family meal taken after 5pm. Classical Danish cuisine comprises meat, often pork, plus potatoes and vegetables such as cabbage and leek, which the nearby nurseries and greenhouses can supply all the year round. It should, however, not be assumed from the list above that Danes, either professionally or privately, do not use rice, noodles or other more exotic vegetables.

79

If you enjoy eating out, then there are plenty of good restaurants to choose from with 130DKK per person the usual starting price. Fish from the Øresund has only a modest reputation, so the restaurateurs have to procure it from further afield and this partly explains why fish menus can be rather expensive. The Scandinavian buffet is also very popular. Guests can eat as much as they like from a range of displayed foods within a chosen price range.

If you want to eat well *and* cheaply, then go to one of the cafés, pubs or restaurants that serve hot meals at lunchtime. The choice of food will not be so great as in the evening, but it will be appetising and filling. Expect to pay 39DKK for the *dagens ret* (dish of the day) including coffee. Many of the newer cafés serve cheap snacks and light meals throughout the day. Copenhagen boasts countless mobile snack bars, which serve *pølser* (sausages) in a variety of ways.

One of many pølser bars

Restaurant selection

The following are recommended restaurants in Copenhagen, listed according to three categories: $$$ (expensive); $$ (moderate); $ (inexpensive).

Gourmet restaurants

Restaurant d'Angleterre, $$$, Kongens Nytorv 34, tel: 33 37 06 43. Open daily 11.30am–11pm. Copenhagen's top hotel and hotel restaurant with an exclusive menu.**Sct. Gertruds Kloster, $$$** , Hauser Plads 32, tel: 33 14 66 30. Open daily 4pm–2am. Grand cellar vaults, illuminated only by candles. **Krogs Fiskerestaurant, $$$,** Gammel Strand 38, tel: 33 15 89 15. Monday to Saturday, 11.30am–4pm and 5.30pm–midnight. Splendid fish restaurant with a view over the Gammel Strand. Bouillabaisse, sole, eel, salmon and lobster served in many forms. **Den Gyldne Fortun, $$$,** Ved Stranden 18, tel: 33 12 20 11. Monday to Friday, noon–3pm and 5–10pm, Saturday and Sunday 6–10pm. By the historic fish market, steep prices but top quality fare. Delicious seafood platter.

Sct. Gertruds Kloster

Danish diners

Delicious dessert

Peder Oxe, $$, Gråbrødretorv 11, tel: 33 11 00 77. Open daily 11.30am–1am. Danish and French cuisine in a row of fine restaurants. Outdoor seating, great salad bar, good wine list. **Det Lille Apotek, $$,** Store Kannikestræde 15, tel: 33 12 56 06. Open Monday to Saturday, 11am–midnight, Sunday noon–midnight. 'The Little Chemist' is a smart city cellar with antique furnishings. Popular with students. **Den Grimme Ælling, $$,** Købmagergade 19, tel: 33 11 20 30. Open daily, noon–2.30pm and 5.30–10.30pm. 'The Ugly Swan' chain specialises in Scandinavian buffets. **Tivoli:** the **Grøften** restaurant, **$$,** (tel: 33 12 11 25) with its red and white check tablecloths is a popular spot. Diners in the more stylish **Balkonen, $$,** (tel: 33 11 27 85) have a pleasant view. Both open daily, noon–3.30am. Danish and French dishes. **Færgekroen, $,** tel: 33 12 94 12. By the sea with an unpretentious seafaring atmosphere. Open daily 11am–midnight.

Frokost restaurants

Ida Davidsen, $–$$, Store Kongensgade 70, tel: 33 91 36 55. Monday to Friday, 9am–5pm. Family-run concern in Frederiksstaden. Large selection. **Caféen i Nikolaj, $–$$,** Nikolay Plads 12, tel: 33 11 63 13. Monday to Saturday, 11.30am–5pm. In a wing of the Nikolaj Church, popular with the locals. Menus and *frokost*. **Sorgenfri, $,** Brolæggerstræde 8, tel: 33 11 58 80. Monday to Saturday, 11am–11pm, Sunday noon–11pm. Central location, serving *smørrebrød* below ground level. Good reputation. **Kongens Kælder, $,** Gothersgade 87, tel: 33 12 87 19. Monday to Saturday, 11am–4pm. Pure *frokost*. Take a list and tick what you want. Good quality food. **Kanal-Kaféen, $,** Frederiksholms Kanal 18, tel: 33 11 57 70. Monday to Friday, 11.30am–7pm. Enjoy a *smørrebrød* in a maritime atmosphere. Herring from the fishing grounds off

Bornholm. **Café & Ølhalle 1892**, **$**, Rømersgade 22, tel: 33 93 25 75. Open daily, 11.30am–4pm. This 'Café and Beer Hall' is part of the Workers' Museum. Original turn-of-the-last-century atmosphere, serving real Danish fare.

Floating Carriage Restaurant

Cafés

Café Sommersko, **$**, Kronprinsensgade 6, tel: 33 14 81 89. Monday to Wednesday, 9am–midnight, Thursday 9–1am, Friday and Saturday 9–2am, Sunday 10am–midnight. The forerunner of the modern café scene. Red sofas give panache. **Cafe Norden**, **$,** Østergade 61, tel: 33 11 77 91. Open daily 9am–midnight. Classic café atmosphere in Art Nouveau style. **Café Klaptræet**, **$**, Kultorvet 11, tel: 33 13 31 48. Monday to Thursday, 10– 2am, Friday, Saturday 10–5am, Sunday 1pm–midnight. Film posters and spotlights are leftovers from its days as a cinema. Popular with young people. **Café Wilder**, **$**, Wildersgade 56, on the corner of Skt Annæ Gade, tel: 31 54 71 83. Monday to Friday, 9–2am, Saturday and Sunday 10–2am. In Christianshavn. Youthful, casual atmosphere behind a glass facade.

For the young crowd

International cuisine

San Giorgio, **$$–$$$**, Rosenborggade 7 (near the Kultorvet), tel: 33 12 61 20. Open daily, 5pm–midnight. Authentic pizza and pasta recipes. **Mongolian Barbecue**,**$$**, Stormgade 35, tel: 33 14 63 20. Open daily, 4pm–midnight. An interesting alternative; at the rear of the National Museum. **Shezan**, **$$**, Viktoriagade 22, tel: 31 24 78 88. Pakistani specialities. **Alanya**, **$–$$,** Vesterbrogade 35, tel: 31 31 92 33. Open daily, noon–midnight. Popular Turkish cuisine. **Bananrepublikken**, **$**, Nørrebrogade 13, tel: 35 36 08 30. Sunday and Monday 11am–midnight, Tuesday 11–2am, Wednesday to Saturday 11–5am. Mainly Mexican and southern European dishes.

A taste of China

What's On

Copenhagen's Tourist Office (*see pages 90–91*) keeps a broad selection of publications but, for the best 'what's on' guide, consult the monthly English-language magazine *Copenhagen This Week*. This handy journal contains additional information about advance ticket sales and exhibitions, has a practical A–Z guide and lists almost every café, pub and restaurant in the city. Note that the 'Late Night' section provides information on those places which serve food until late into the night; it is not a list of nightclubs.

One handy tip: the Royal Theatre box office offers 50 percent reductions on unsold tickets for events taking place that day from 5pm onwards. For as little as 25DKK, it may be possible to buy a ticket for a performance at the Royal Theatre, as long it's not an extravagant production with increased admission prices.

The Royal Theatre

Det Kongelige Teater

The Royal Theatre by Kongens Nytorv (1874) provides a home for three different art forms: drama, opera and ballet. While plays in Danish may not have much appeal for foreign visitors, it is definitely worth enquiring about tickets for opera or ballet performances. Advance ticket sales Monday to Friday.

The Copenhagen Royal Ballet Company has a particularly good reputation. Vicenzo Galeotti (1775–1816), August Bournonville (1833–77) and Harald Lander (balletmaster at the Royal Danish Ballet School from 1932 to 1951) were all innovative figures on the Danish ballet scene. Lander engaged classical and avant-garde dancers and, in so doing, quickly enhanced the Royal Ballet's international reputation.

Performance posters

Classical music

Tivoli Koncertsalen, Vesterbrogade 3, tel: 33 15 10 12. Advance ticket sales: Monday to Friday 9am–7pm, Saturday and Sunday 10am–7pm. The Concert Hall in the pleasure gardens is home to the Tivoli Symphony Orchestra, which accompany singing groups, guest musicians and conductors. Foreign orchestras also perform here. Separate entrance from the Tietgensgade. Some concerts free.

Church music

Concerts take place in Copenhagen's churches throughout the year and the vast majority of them are free – an admirable tradition. Ask in the Tourist Office for the concert programme, which is published every three or four months. While it is written in Danish, the basic information will be perfectly understandable without any knowledge of the language.

Jazz clubs

Copenhagen Jazz House, Niels Hemmingsensgade, tel: 33 15 26 00. Open for concerts 6pm–midnight, disco Thursday to Saturday, midnight–5am. As the city's top venue, this club attracts talent from throughout Denmark and beyond. Prime location in the city-centre near the Helligaandskirken.

Tivoli Jazzhouse, Tivoli, Vesterbrogade, tel: 33 11 11 13. Monday to Saturday 9pm–2am. Traditional jazz provided by several long-serving Copenhagen players. Separate entrance from the Bernstorffgade.

Finn Zieglers Hjørne, Vodroffsvej 24, tel: 31 24 54 54. Monday to Saturday 9pm–2am. Small, intimate jazz bar with good restaurant, live music every evening. For details, see the notice board at the entrance. In Frederiksberg, near Skt Jørgens Lake.

Rock, blues and folk

Pumpehuset, Studiestræde 52, near Axeltorv, tel: 33 93 19 60. Daily 8pm–5am. This old waterworks (1859) is Copenhagen's top venue for rock music.

Mojo Blues Bar, Løngangsstræde 21C, tel: 33 11 64 53. Daily 8pm–5am. Blues more often than rock. Between City Hall Square and the National Museum.

Shamrock Inn, Jernbanegade 9, tel: 33 14 06 02. Sunday to Wednesday 11am–2am, Thursday 11am–3am, Friday, Saturday 11am–5am. Irish Folk washed down with Guinness. In the Scala Building by Axeltorv.

During the summer months, **Fælledpark**, north of the city centre in the Østerbro district, is often used for open-air concerts (from soul to country music).

Coming up at the Tivoli

Street music

Dancing

Bananrepublikken, Nørrebrogade 13, tel: 35 36 08 30. Sunday to Monday 11am–midnight, Tuesday 11–2am, Wednesday to Saturday 11–5am. In the Nørrebro district. Salsa and Latin rhythms preferred. Live music.

Rust, Guldbergsgæde, tel: 35 24 52 00. Monday to Saturday 5.30pm–5am. Late night disco with café and bar. Live music, rock and on Wednesdays techno, otherwise mixed programme.

Woodstock, Vestergade 12, by Axeltorv, tel: 33 11 20 71. Thursday 9pm–5am, Friday and Saturday 10pm–5am. '60s and '70s music not just for oldies.

Blue Note , Studiestræde 31, tel: 33 13 08 06. Friday and Saturday 5pm–5am. Mainly techno and house.

Late-night venue

Light night snacks

Pasta Basta, Valkendorffsgade 22, tel: 33 11 21 31. Sunday to Thursday 11.30am–3am, Frida and Saturday 11.30am–5am. Pasta buffets and delicious salads – even after midnight. Reasonable prices. Central location.

Red lights

Copenhagen's reputation as a sex metropolis began in 1969, when Denmark lifted the ban on pornography. Many of the sex shops that opened at the time to satisfy mainly foreign visitors have now closed, but Copenhagen still beats Hamburg or Amsterdam as the sex capital of Europe.

Funfairs

Tivoli, Vesterbrogade 3. 1 May to 15 September, Sunday to Wednesday 11am–midnight, Thursday to Saturday 11–1am. The famous Tivoli Gardens (*see Route 1*) is not just a fairground and park, it also provides a stage for symphony concerts, jazz, pop, variety artists and pantomime.

Welcome to Bakken

Bakken, Dyrehavsbakken, Klampenborg. End March to end August, daily 2pm–midnight. Free admission. Occupying a part the former royal hunting grounds of Klampenborg, less than 30 minutes' drive to the north of the city, this amusement park (*see Excursion 1, pages 65–6*) claims to be the world's oldest and is more down-to-earth than the sophisticated Tivoli. Rides and stalls. Pieter Lieps' rustic restaurant in the forest is where the locals go for a romantic summer rendezvous.

Zoo København, Roskildevej 32, tel: 36 30 20 01. 1 November to 28 February, daily 9am–4pm; March Monday to Friday 9am–4pm, Saturday and Sunday 9am–5pm, 1 April to 31 May, Monday to Friday 9am–5pm, Saturday and Sunday 9am–6pm; 1 June to 31 August, daily 9am–6pm; 1 September to 31 October, daily 9am–5pm. Situated in Frederiksberg (*see Route 8, page 60*), this is a very popular destination for family days out.

Shopping

Shopping streets

Linking Rådhuspladsen with Kongens Nytorv, the city's main shopping area takes in five streets and squares. Frederiksberggade, Nygade, Vimmelskaftet, Amagertorv and Østergade are known collectively as **Strøget**, or the 'Strip'. Many of the shops here are exclusive. The streets around **Fiolstræde**, which branches off Strøget near the Vimmelskaftet, are less grand. Here, in the university quarter, the range includes a number of antiquarian bookshops.

Department stores

Magasin du Nord, Kongens Nytorv 13. A shoppers' paradise behind a Renaissance facade. Usually known simply as the 'Magasin'.

Illum, Østergade 52. The second-largest department store giant with a reputation for quality. Antiques market on the second floor, plus a good restaurant on the roof terrace.

Danish design

Illums Bolighus, Amagertorv 10. A furnishing company with its finger on the fashion pulse.

Illums Bolighus

85

Georg Jensen, Amagertorv 4. Internationally renowned silversmith since 1904. Jewellery, cutlery and chandeliers.

Royal Copenhagen, Amagertorv 6. Porcelain and glass, ornaments and everyday objects.

Holmegaard, Østergade 15. Fine glassware manufacturer in southern Sealand (1825).

Bang & Olufsen, Østergade 3–5. Hi-fi equipment with visual appeal. Worth a visit, even if only to browse.

Fashion

Boutiques, such as those in the **Scala Building** by Axeltorv, always keep up with the times. Also try the boutiques in **Skt Peders Stræde** and **Lars Bjørns Stræde** in the north-west of the city.

Bang & Olufsen

Antiques

Quality antiques shops are concentrated mainly in the **Farvergade**, **Kompagnistræde** and **Læderstræde** areas.

Flea markets

Loppemarked takes place from May to September. The markets listed below are held on a regular basis. Consult the 'Wonderful Copenhagen' events calendar for a full list.

Gammel Strand. Saturday and Sunday 8am–2pm. Includes good-quality antiques.

Israel Plads. Saturday 8am–2pm. Typical flea market.

Frederiksberg, Smallegade. Saturday 8am–2pm. On the square behind Frederiksberg Town Hall.

Getting There

By plane
Copenhagen airport is situated to the east of the town on Amager Island. Scheduled flights arrive daily from most European countries. A shuttle service with three to six buses every hour links Kastrup and Copenhagen's central station; journey time about 25 minutes.

By train
Trains arrive daily from Germany, Britain and Sweden. Hovedbanegården, the central station, is situated opposite Tivoli and the Tourist Office. Buses for onward journeys leave either from outside the station or the nearby City Hall Square. The S-trains leaving from the central station run on a separate network. For rail information, tel: 33 14 17 01.

By bus
Several bus companies on mainland Europe operate services to the Danish capital. Although the bus from Hamburg – the nearest large German city to the Danish border – takes six hours, it works out much cheaper than the train. The buses stop outside Copenhagen's central station. For timetable information in Copenhagen, contact Eurolines Skandinavia, Reventolwsgade 8, tel: 33 25 12 44.

87

By boat
Copenhagen is easily accessible by sea. The main ferry crossings to Denmark from Germany are Puttgarden and Rødby, Kiel and Bagenkop, Travemünde and Gedser. There are also numerous services from Norway and Sweden. Car ferries to Denmark from Britain leave Harwich and dock in Esbjerg on the west coast. During the summer months, Esbjerg can also be reached by car ferry from Newcastle. It can pay to make reservations for a vehicle for both domestic and international ferry routes as early as possible.

Ferry services are plentiful

By car
Most British visitors to Denmark arrive either by ferry direct from the UK or from Germany, and then either on the motorway from Hamburg in the west or by car ferry across the Femer Bælt from Puttgarden to Rødby. A good motorway, the E47, covers the last 165km (102 miles) to Copenhagen. Boats leave Puttgarden throughout the day practically every half hour and the journey takes just under an hour. You don't normally have to wait very long, except on busy summer weekends. Traffic can also be heavy at these times on the main road border crossing north of Flensburg.

Getting Around

Parking

If you want to stop, you have to pay. There are four different colour-coded zones within Greater Copenhagen and, depending on which one you use, you can expect to pay between 5 and 20DKK to park your car. The closer to the city centre, the higher the charges. In the red zone, the most expensive, the maximum stay is three hours, otherwise 10 hours. Machines supply the parking slip. Charges apply on weekdays from 8am to 6pm, and on Saturday in the red and yellow zone from 8am to 2pm. If you find one of the few free parking places, then you must display a parking disc. Unless otherwise stated, one hour is the maximum stay.

So the case for using the buses and the S-trains is easily made. Sightseers will find that buying a 'Copenhagen Card' makes good sense (*see page 89*).

By bus

The bus network is extensive

The bus network covers practically every destination and must be the best way to get around. Nearly all buses stop at either City Hall Square and Kongens Nytorv.

Passengers enter at the front and alight at the rear, with the driver selling the tickets. The urban area is divided into zones and the pricing system is rather complicated, so just tell the driver where you want to go. The Copenhagen Card (*see page 89*) or a period ticket, valid for one day (70DKK), can be used in every zone in the network. Show your ticket when entering the bus.

S-trains run underground

By S-train

The S-train connects Copenhagen with the suburbs and other towns on Sealand. Within the city, it runs underground. The main stations in the city, apart from the central railway station are, from north to south, Vesterport, Nørreport and Østerport. Tickets available at all S-stations.

Cyclists enjoy equal status

By bicycle

Cyclists enjoy equal status with motorists on Copenhagen's roads and consequently they usually make rapid and relatively safe progress on what is a dense cycle network. Cyclists have their own traffic lights at tricky junctions. When using the cycleways, keep to the right.

If you don't have your own bike, hire one of the 'City Bikes'. You will see these sturdy two-wheelers around the city. They are stored in racks at 120 different places around Copenhagen and can be released with a 20-*krone* coin. You get your money back when you return it to any one of the racks. Look in *Copenhagen This Week* for the addresses of bike hire companies.

The Copenhagen Card

The Copenhagen Card or 'CC' grants free admission to almost all museums, castles and other sights, free travel on buses and S-trains and reductions on certain sightseeing trips. It costs 155DKK for 24 hours, 255DKK for 48 hours and 320DKK for 72 hours. Children pay 70.50, 127.50 and 160DKK respectively. When you purchase the card, it is stamped with the starting date and the user enters the time it is first used. As well as the ticket and a map of the city, you also receive a booklet which shows details of each attraction's opening times and public transport connections.

The card may be purchased from the Tourist Office, at most hotels, travel agents, stations and at the airport.

Children pay half fare

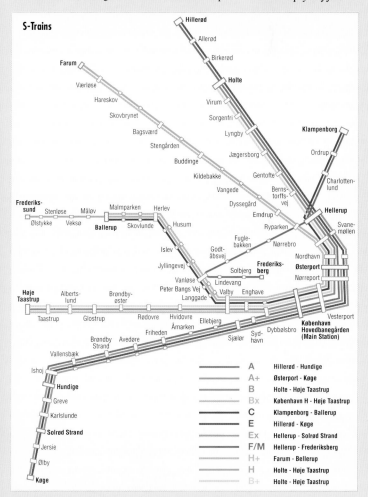

	A	Hillerød - Hundige
	A+	Østerport - Køge
	B	Holte - Høje Taastrup
	Bx	København H - Høje Taastrup
	C	Klampenborg - Ballerup
	E	Hillerød - Køge
	Ex	Hellerup - Solrød Strand
	F/M	Hellerup - Frederiksberg
	H+	Farum - Ballerup
	H	Holte - Høje Taastrup
	B+	Holte - Høje Taastrup

A break in the itinerary

Facts for the Visitor

Travel documents

Most visitors – including citizens of the UK, USA, Canada, Éire, Australia and New Zealand – need only a passport, which is valid for at least three months at time of entry.

A useful port of call

Customs

Since the abolition of the duty-free system within the European Union, if you are an EU visitor you may buy as much as you like during your journey, provided it is for your own use. If you bring back more than the following guidance levels for consumer goods, customs may ask you to show the goods are for your own use: 800 cigarettes, 200 cigars, 1kg of tobacco, 90 litres of wine, 10 litres of spirit and 100 litres of beer per person.

'Duty-frees' are still available to travellers to and from countries outside the EU.

Tourist information

When planning your holiday, contact the Danish Tourist Board who will supply leaflets and brochures etc.

In the UK: The Danish Tourist Board, 55 Sloane Street, London SW1X 9SY, tel: 0171 259 5959. There is also a special information line for requesting information packs on Denmark and Copenhagen, tel: 09001 600109.
In the US: The Danish Tourist Board, 655 Third Avenue, 18th floor, New York, NY 10017, tel: 212 885 9700; Scandinavian Tourist Board, 150 North Michigan Avenue, Suite 2110, Chicago, IL 60601, tel: 312 726 1120; Scandinavian Tourist Board, 8929 Wiltshire Boulevard, Beverly Hills, CA 90211, tel: 213 854 1549.

Information in Copenhagen available from Københavns Turistinformation, Bernstorffsgade 1, 1577 København V, tel: 33 11 13 25, fax: 33 93 49 69.

The following are provided free of charge: city map, what's on guide, information on sightseeing, transport, dining out, obtaining English-speaking guides and reservation of concert and theatre tickets. Hotel reservations (*see page 94*) are arranged for a small fee, however, you can't do this over the telephone. The office is situated between Tivoli Gardens and the central station. Open 1 May to 31 August, Monday to Saturday 9am–8pm, Sunday 10am–8pm; otherwise Monday to Friday 9am–4.30pm, Saturday 9am–1.30pm.

Wonderful Copenhagen, the official website run by the convention and visitors bureau of the Greater Copenhagen region (www.woco.dk) contains all you need to know about the city and offers useful links to other sites.

Use It, Youth Tourist Information, Rådhusstræde 13, 1466 København K, tel: 33 73 06 19, fax: 33 73 06 20. Meeting place for young people 10 minutes from City Hall Square. Information on budget accommodation and restaurants, sightseeing, events and lifts. Open 15 June to 14 September, daily 9am–7pm; otherwise Monday to Wednesday 11am–4pm, Thursday 11am–6pm, Friday 10am–2pm.

Currency
The *krone* (DKK) is the Danish currency. 1 *krone* = 100 *øre*. You will find notes to the value of 50, 100, 500 and 1,000 *krone*, coins at 1, 2, 5, 10 and 20 *krone*, plus 25 and 50 *øre*, but *øre* are usually rounded up or down. Most banks have 24-hour teller machines (look for the word *Kontanten*) and you can draw out up to 3,000DKK with Eurocheque cards and some credit cards, but expect to pay a commission whether you use the machine or cash a cheque at the counter.

Krone are easily obtained

Eurocheques can be used for payments up to 1,500 DKK. There are no restrictions on importing and exporting currencies.

Sightseeing tours
City walks
Two-hour guided tours of the central area with English-speaking guide. Meet in the Tourist Office. 1 May to 30 September at 10.30am. Price: 40DKK. Tel: 32 97 14 40.

Sightseeing by bus

Bus tours
Start in City Hall Square, tel: 32 54 06 06. Children half-price. Short tours: duration: 1hr 30 mins. 15 May to 15 June, daily at 9.30am and 3pm; 1 June to 15 September, daily at 9.30am, 1pm, and 3pm. Fare: 125DKK.

City and harbour tours (part of tour by boat): duration 2hrs 30 mins. 15 May to 15 June, daily at 9.30am; 16 June to 15 September, daily at 9.30am, 1pm and 3pm. Fare: 135DKK. Copenhagen Excursions, tel: 32 54 06 06. This Tour can be booked at the Tourist Information office.

Grand tour of Copenhagen with visit to Langelinie, Gefion Fountain and Amalienborg: duration: 2hrs 30 mins. 1 April to 30 September, daily at 11am and 1.30pm; otherwise daily at 11am, Sunday at 1.30pm. Fare: 160DKK. Auto Paaske, tel: 32 57 26 00.

Castle Tour of North Sealand: duration: 7 hrs. 1 May to 15 October, Wednesday, Saturday and Sunday at 10.15am; otherwise Wednesday and Sunday at 10.15am. Fare: 335DKK. Price of lunch not included. Auto Paaske, tel: 32 57 26 00.

Harbour and canal tours
Canal tours: duration: 1 hr. Leave from Gammel Strand, Nyhavn, Little Mermaid. Beginning of April until end of September, daily 10am–5pm; 20 June to 10 August, until 7.30pm. Departures every half hour with multi-lingual commentary. Fare: 42DKK. Canal Tours, tel: 33 13 31 05.

Water bus: duration: 1 hr. Leave from Gammel Strand, Nyhavn. Little Mermaid. 1 May to 30 September, daily 10.15am–4.45pm. Departures every half hour. No guide. Fare: 25DKK. 1 June to 31 August, from the Little Mermaid to Trekronor Fortress in the Øresund; supplement payable.

Seeing the city from the canals

Tipping

A cash tip is customary

Restaurant bills include a service charge, but many customers reward good service with a cash tip. Taxi drivers do not regard a tip as essential, just a pleasant bonus.

Opening times

Opening times in Denmark are not strictly regulated and the following should be regarded only as guidelines. Many shops on Strøget are open on Sundays.

Banks: Monday to Friday 9.30am–4pm, Thursday until 6pm.

Souvenir guards

Post offices: Monday to Friday 9/10am–5/6pm, Saturday 9am–noon/1pm.

Shops: Monday to Wednesday 9/10am–5.30/6pm, Thursday, Friday until 7/8pm, Saturday until noon/1/2pm.

Public holidays

Banks, offices and most shops close on New Year's Day, Maundy Thursday, Good Friday, Easter Sunday, Easter Monday, May Day, General Prayer Day (Store Bededag), on the fourth Friday after Easter, Ascension Day, Whit

Sunday, Whit Monday, Constitution Day on 5 June, 25 and 26 December.

Telephone

Not all phones have cabins

Coin- and card-operated telephone kiosks can be found in all parts of Copenhagen, but most are open to the elements and sometimes it is not easy to carry on a normal conversation, particularly in busy city centre locations. 1, 2, 5 and 10DKK coins, and cards to the value of 20, 50, 100DKK are accepted. The latter may be bought from all post offices and most pavement kiosks.

To phone the UK, dial 00+44+local code without the zero+number. You will have to insert at least 5DKK. Eight-digit numbers (without codes) apply throughout Denmark, with 2DKK the minimum charge for a local call. To call Denmark from abroad, dial 00+45+number.

Medical

Citizens of EU countries are entitled to free medical treatment in Danish hospitals on production of the E111 document. For minor complaints, however, patients pay the doctor or dentist at the time of treatment and then claim the fees back from the local health service offices. The staff at the Tourist Office will provide the address and also offer guidance on the choice of doctor. It is nevertheless advisable to take out a private medical and accident insurance policy to cover all eventualities.

Medicines are available from chemists (*apotek*) and a prescription is not always necessary. Steno Apotek, Vesterbrogade 6, tel: 33 14 82 66, provides a 24-hour service.

Disabled

Public buildings such as post offices, museums and hotels normally provide good facilities for the disabled. A booklet available from the Danish Tourist Board (*see pages 90–1*) offers information for disabled users of public transport, hotels, restaurants and tourist sights.

Emergencies

For police, fire-brigade and ambulance, dial 112. Free from phone boxes.

Routine patrol

Lost and found

Police at Slotsherrensvej 113, Vanløse, tel: 38 74 88 22. Monday to Thursday 9am–5.30pm, Friday 9am–2pm.

Diplomatic representation

British Embassy, Kaftlevej 36–40, 2100 Copenhagen 0, tel: 35 26 46 000.
US Embassy, Dag Hammarskjölds Allé 24, 2100 Copenhagen 0, tel: 31 42 31 44.

Accommodation

Hotels near the main station

When you are looking around for accommodation, a number of factors have to be weighed up. A centrally-located hotel can save time and money when visiting the main sights and the public transport system is very efficient. On the other hand, the city-centre hotels do not usually have car parks.

Generally speaking, it is better to use the room-finding service offered by the Tourist Office (*see pages 90–1*). You state your requirements and the computer finds a suitable room. If you are visiting the city off-season, you can often save a sizeable sum off the normal price, because hotels offer reduced rates to fill their empty rooms.

Many of the larger hotels that have facilities for conferences and meetings make reductions at the weekend or during the holiday season. Breakfast is included in the published price, unless otherwise stated.

Hotel selection

The following selection of Copenhagen hotels are divided into three categories: $$$ = expensive; $$ = moderate; $ = inexpensive.

$$$

Hotel d'Angleterre

Hotel d'Angleterre, Kongens Nytorv 34, 1050 Copenhagen K, tel: 33 12 00 95, fax: 33 12 11 18. The wealthy, the important and the beautiful take refuge behind the grand facade. Elegant rooms with a rather stiff, old-fashioned atmosphere. **Copenhagen Admiral Hotel**, Toldbodgade 24–28, 1253 Copenhagen K, tel: 33 11 82 82, fax: 33 32 55 42. Two old warehouses have merged and have been restored with exposed beams. Fine view over the Øresund. **71 Nyhavn Hotel**, Nyhavn 71, 1051 Copenhagen K, tel: 33 11 85 85, fax: 33 93 15 85. Expensively renovated warehouse. By the waterside with great view of Nyhavn, Sund and ferry terminal.

$$

Hotel Christian IV, Dronningens Tværgade 45, 1302 Copenhagen K, tel: 33 32 10 44, fax: 33 32 07 06. Centrally located near Rosenborg Have. Pleasant atmosphere. Quiet rooms with window overlooking courtyard. **Park Hotel**, Jarmers Plads 3, 1551 Copenhagen V, tel: 33 13 30 00, fax: 33 14 30 33. By the busy Ørstedsparken. Only 10-minute walk to City Hall Square. Large, tastefully furnished rooms. **Hotel Esplanaden**, Bredgade 78, 1260 Copenhagen K, tel: 33 96 20 02, fax: 33 96 20 97. Bright, high-ceilinged rooms behind an impressive, classical facade. The choice of furnishings was apparently based on a survey carried out among guests. **Hotel Cosmopole**, Colbjørnsensgade 5–11, 1652 Copenhagen V, tel: 33 21 33 33, fax: 33 31 33 99. Noisy nightclubs for neighbours but, situated near the station, it has the best location in this category. Some spacious rooms.

$

Hotel Cab Inn Scandinavia, Vodroffsvej 55, 1900 Frederiksberg C, tel: 35 36 11 11, fax: 35 36 11 14. Unusual rooms rather like ferry cabins. In Frederiksberg near Skt Jørgens Lake and only 15 minutes from the city centre. **Bertrams Hotel**, Vesterbrogade 107, 1602 Copenhagen V, tel: 33 25 04 05, fax: 33 25 04 02. On the main street through Vesterbro. Intimate hotel with friendly rooms and possibly Copenhagen's narrowest lift.

Youth hostels

Copenhagen Danhostel Amager, Sjællandsbroen 55, 2300 Copenhagen S, tel: 32 52 29 08, fax: 32 52 27 08. 15 January to 30 November. 528 beds. The most modern of the youth hostels in a thinly-populated corner of Amager Island. Bus no. 46 or 37, then 16. **Copenhagen Danhostel Bellahøj**, Herbergvejen 8, Bellahøj, 2700 Bronshøj, tel: 38 28 97 15, fax: 38 89 02 10. 1 March to 15 January. 250 beds. Typical hostel-type building, which has probably seen better days, but then it is not far from the city centre. Bus no. 2. **Danhostel Lyngby-Tårbæk Vandrerhjem**, Rådvad 1, 2800 Lyngby, tel: 45 80 30 74. 1 April to 25 October. 94 beds. Small and friendly. Quite a long way from the city centre, but in the Lyngby recreational area. Not easy to reach. S-train to Lyngby, bus to Hjortekær, and then a 15-minute walk.

Lyngby-Tårbæk Vandrerhjem youth hostel

95

Camping

Apart from Charlottenlund, all camp sites rent out cabins. These make good stand-bys in poor weather. **Bellahøj Camping**, Hvidkildevej, Bronshøj, tel: 38 10 11 50. 1 June to 31 August. The only camp-site within easy reach of the city centre. Large grassy area with modest toilet facilities. A popular meeting place for young people in summer. Bus no. 11 or 12. **Charlottenlund Strandpark**, Strandvejen 144B, Charlottenlund, tel: 39 62 36 88. 15 May to 15 September. On the site of an old fortification. Pleasant green space right by the coast. Cramped but friendly. S-train to Copenhagen. **Absalon Camping**, Korsdalsvej 132, Rødovre, tel: 36 41 06 00. Open all year. Large site with enclosed pitches. Close to the E47 motorway, otherwise fine. Bus no. 550 S. **Tangloppen**, Tangloppen 2, Ishøj Havn, tel: 43 54 07 67. 1 May to 15 September. The quietest camp site near the city centre. On a headland in Køge Strandpark. Relaxed maritime atmosphere. Bus no. 128 to Ishøj S-station.

The outdoor option

Index